Money
and
Marriage
GOD'S WAY

Money
and
Marriage
GOD'S WAY

HOWARD DAYTON

MOODY PUBLISHERS
CHICAGO

All Scripture quotations, unless otherwise indicated, are taken from the *Holy Bible, New International Version*®. NIV®. Copyright © 1973, 1978, 1984 by International Bible Society. Used by permission of Zondervan. All rights reserved.

Scripture quotations marked NASB are taken from the *New American Standard Bible®*, Copyright © 1960, 1962, 1963, 1968, 1971, 1972, 1973, 1975, 1977, 1995 by The Lockman Foundation. Used by permission. (www.Lockman.org).

Scripture quotations marked MSG are from *The Message*, copyright © by Eugene H. Peterson 1993, 1994, 1995. Used by permission of NavPress Publishing Group.

Scripture quotations marked KJV are taken from the King James Version.

Scripture quotations marked NKJV are taken from the *New King James Version*. Copyright © 1982 by Thomas Nelson, Inc. Used by permission. All rights reserved.

Scripture quotations marked TLB are taken from *The Living Bible* copyright © 1971. Used by permission of Tyndale House Publishers, Inc., Wheaton, Illinois 60189. All rights reserved.

Scripture quotations marked NLT are taken from the *Holy Bible, New Living Translation*, copyright © 1996, 2004. Used by permission of Tyndale House Publishers, Inc., Wheaton, Illinois 60189, U.S.A. All rights reserved.

The Crown Money Map™ and MoneyLife™ are trademarked terms.

Emphases added to Scripture have been placed by the author.

Editors: Larry Libby and Pam Pugh
Cover Design: Paetzold Associates
Cover Image:: iStockphoto
Interior Design: Smartt Guys design

Library of Congress Cataloging-in-Publication Data
Dayton, Howard Lape, 1943-
    Money and marriage God's way / Howard Dayton.
        p. cm.
    Includes bibliographical references.
    ISBN 978-0-8024-2258-3
    1. Marriage—Religious aspects—Christianity. 2. Finance, Personal—
Religious aspects—Christianity. I. Title. II. Title: Money and marriage God's way.

BV835.D395 2009
241'.6808655–dc22

2008044470

This book is printed on acid free recycled paper containing 30% PCW (Post Consumer Waste) and manufactured in the United States of America by Bethany Press.

We hope you enjoy this book from Moody Publishers. Our goal is to provide high-quality, thought-provoking books and products that connect truth to your real needs and challenges. For more information on other books and products written and produced from a biblical perspective, go to www.moodypublishers.com or write to:

Moody Publishers
820 N. LaSalle Boulevard
Chicago, IL 60610

3 5 7 9 10 8 6 4 2

Printed in the United States of America

To Bev Dayton

My wife, best friend, life partner, and hero.

When we first married, you promised our lives together
would not be boring—you were so right!
You have changed me by your prayers and love.

Acknowledgments

I'm especially grateful to Larry Libby for his wonderful skill in bringing the message of *Money and Marriage God's Way* to life.

Ron Deal, Steve Gardner, Kevin Light, Bob Lepine, Steve Lyon, Don and Sally Meredith, Steve and Laura Petherbridge, Greg Pettys, Dr. Brad Pierce, Gary and Barb Rosberg, and Mitch Temple . . . thank you for sharing your passion for healthy marriages and finances, and your God-given insight on how to achieve them.

Raymond and Marydel Harris, Bill and Christy Heavener, Jim and Sally Phillips, and Jim and Ann Tharp . . . thank you for your remarkable friendship and hospitality.

Gray and Dixie Fraley Keller and JD Gibbs and the Joe Gibbs Racing team . . . thank you for your vision and generosity in helping to make this a reality.

Chuck Bentley, Sharon Epps, Dave Rae, and Stan Reiff—thank you for your commitment to lead Crown Financial Ministries in a way that pleases God.

Lord Jesus Christ . . . thank You for creating marriage and for giving us the keys to enjoy successful ones.

Contents

Let's Start:

GETTING THE MOST FROM THIS BOOK

This book will transform your marriage and your finances.

"Well, Howard," you say, "that's a pretty big claim. How can you make such a statement?"

Here's how.

As you begin to learn what the God of the universe has to say about having a great marriage and successfully handling money—and then put those principles to work in your life—you *will* be transformed.

God is in the life-transforming business, and nobody but nobody does it better.

Money and Marriage is for engaged couples and for everyone who is married—whether newly married or empty nesters, whether you earn a lot or a little. It is designed to help couples experiencing a marital crisis or those who simply want to improve an already good marriage.

I urge you to read through the entire book to understand the big picture of what God wants you to know about marriage and money. Then, carefully reread the chapters addressing your particular situation.

We've all had the experience of reading books, and then a few days later, we can barely remember what we just read.

Don't let *this* book be one of *those* books.

The twin subject matters here—money and marriage—are too important to take lightly. We're not just talking about dollars and cents here . . . we're not just talking about credit cards, budgets, and number-crunching; we're talking about *lives*. We're talking about the precious lives of your wife or husband and your children and grandchildren—and perhaps of generations to come.

How you handle your marriage in the context of finances—and how you handle your finances in the context of marriage—will go a long way toward determining whether or not you will have a life that is really worth living.

For that reason, I urge you to read this book, but more than that, to *consume* this book. Have you ever seen a book read by someone who really valued and appreciated the contents? It's usually a mess! Its pages are underlined, highlighted, creased, and dog-eared. It has writing in the margins—and maybe even ketchup or coffee stains on the cover.

I hope this one looks like that someday. I pray you not only read it, but personalize it. Underline it. Write notes in it. Make it *yours*. The books that have helped me the most are the ones that I interacted with, not just quickly read.

If this book ends up back on your bookshelf with clean and perfect pages and a cover still bearing the original bookstore gloss, I will not have accomplished my desire.

Study this book with your spouse, or better yet, become part of a small group to encourage one another to apply what you are learning.

Money and Marriage God's Way includes these features to assist you as you make progress in your marriage and in your financial life:

1. React: Let's talk about it. The book is divided into six sections, and at the end of each you'll find questions to talk about. Meet with your spouse or a group to answer the questions, discuss what you read, and bounce ideas off each other. This will help you. No, let me restate that—this will help you *enormously*.

2. Help!—Online and other resources. At the end of each section, you will find tools you can access online. In addition, we have identified for you outstanding books, marriage and financial materials, and organizations that are among the best available to help you.

3. Encouragement from a couple you should know. Read true stories of couples who applied the principles found in this book to challenging situations.

Got a question about money? We want to help you. Each week thousands of people seek answers to their financial questions online on Crown's Web site. Go to MoneyandMarriage.org to ask or research your question. We may even answer it on an upcoming *MoneyLife* radio program!

Also included in this book are some of the most common questions we've received concerning marriage and money.

As I wrote this book, I often prayed you would experience the awesome sense of hope, peace, and confidence that comes from discovering God's way of having a successful marriage and handling money wisely. I am excited because I know great things are going to happen to you. They happened to my wife, Bev, and me, and we have never been the same.

So, let's get started together.

part one

Marriage

ONCE AND FOR ALL

"For my thoughts are not your thoughts,
neither are your ways my ways,"
declares the Lord.

"As the heavens are higher than the earth,
so are my ways higher than your ways
and my thoughts than your thoughts."

ISAIAH 55:8–9

1

"We Need...
HELP!"

George Sullivan went numb. Then waves of fear flooded over him.

He picked up the note from his wife, Michelle, and read it again in complete disbelief. She told him she still loved him, but the stress of constant arguments over their finances was more than she could bear. She needed space, maybe separation . . . and, if things didn't improve, perhaps even a divorce.

George broke out in a cold sweat. He felt like he'd been punched in the stomach and was fighting to catch his breath. Ten years of marriage and three children later it had come to this? Where could he turn for help? Who could he talk to about rescuing his marriage? His mind was spinning.

Suddenly, he thought about their neighbors, the Daytons. They got along so well, and Michelle had said that they had a good handle on their money. She had tried to get George to open up to them, but, *Why was I so stubborn? Why didn't I agree with Michelle to meet them?* he thought.

Knowing he had nothing to lose, he picked up his phone and speed-dialed Michelle's cell. When he heard her voice, his own nearly failed him. Emotions slammed into him like a Georgia cloudburst.

"Michelle . . . " he finally said. "Hi, it's me."

There was a silence on the other end of the line.

"I . . . I want our marriage to work," he stammered. "Okay, we need help. I know that now."

"And . . . ?" Michelle said, finally speaking.

"I'm willing to go to someone for help . . . like the Daytons. Okay with you?"

"I wouldn't mind," she said. "It's a step anyway."

Relief washed over George, leaving him weak in the knees.

Later that evening the Sullivans met with us in our living room. It was clear that their relationship was in trouble. As they described their situation, they couldn't even look at each other. George was embarrassed. Michelle swung between hurt and anger.

They lived paycheck to paycheck, had a pile of debt, and very little money saved. Despite repeated promises that he would spend carefully, George often spent impulsively without discussing his purchases with Michelle. She felt betrayed and no longer trusted him.

"Every time we talk about our finances or even sit down to work out the bills, we end up in a huge fight. I'm tired of it," Michelle declared. "It's affected every area of our marriage—and I mean every area. I can't live like this anymore."

"You're not alone in struggling with money," I said, searching for the right words to reply to this deeply troubled couple. "In fact, it's the number one thing couples argue about."

"That's right," my wife, Bev, added. "Early in our marriage, Howard and I often fought over money. And sometimes it got pretty ugly. But all that began to change once we learned what God says about both marriage and money."

What you learn will often seem radical and revolutionary

It was as if a little light went on in the midst of George's gloom. "God says something about marriage and about money?" he said. "You mean like—He says stuff about credit card debt and falling behind on our car payments?"

Bev laughed, and some of the tension in the room lifted a little. "Well, God doesn't talk about credit cards or auto loans," she said. "But He does give us basic truths that will strengthen and improve any marriage."

She glanced over at me with a smile. "And Howard and I are living proof of what can happen when someone learns these principles."

"That's right," I affirmed. "God loves you and cares deeply for you and He knows money is a big part of our lives. That's why the Bible has so much to say about it—would you be surprised if I told you money is mentioned more than two thousand times in the Bible?"

"Really?" George said.

"Sure, God knows that money would be a struggle for all of us in our lives and marriages, and He wants to equip us to handle it well."

"I never knew that," Michelle commented.

"God wants you to use money and even money challenges to bring the two of you closer to each other rather than damaging your marriage," I continued. "Most couples view money as a wedge that divides them—and for a lot of couples it is—but God intends money to be one of the glues that bonds your love for each other."

"And the Bible is equally practical when it comes to how to have a great marriage," Bev added. "God designed marriage to be a blessing."

George leaned back in his chair a little. "Well," he said flatly, "our marriage is in trouble—and our finances are pretty much a wreck. I have no clue what the Bible says about all this, but . . . I'm willing to learn if it will help us. You too, Michelle?"

"You *know* I'm ready," she replied.

Your financial life and marriage may not be in as critical shape as that of George and Michelle—or it might be worse. But the truths from the Bible that you will learn in this book will improve your marriage and your finances. You might be surprised to know that money and possessions are actually mentioned more than 2,350 times in the Bible, and that 15 percent of everything Jesus said had to do with this topic!

However, I need to warn you: what you learn will often seem

radical and revolutionary because it's so different from the way most couples view their marriages and their finances. But what you learn can transform your relationship and your financial statement—for the better. As I said, I can guarantee that because you will be learning what the Lord of the universe knows is best for you.

God expressed it this way in Isaiah 55:8–9: "'My thoughts are not your thoughts, neither are your ways my ways,' declares the Lord. 'As the heavens are higher than the earth, so are my ways higher than your ways and my thoughts than your thoughts.'"

God has His ways, and they are the best ways. But they're not always the ways our culture accepts. God has paths for us to walk, and they are very good paths. But they're not always the ones that most people follow. God's ways of having a terrific marriage and stable finances are very different from the way most people think and act. But they are so much higher—so much better—than most people can even imagine.

Bev and I will be transparent and share our own journey with you. When we were newly married, issues over money were harming our relationship. We didn't know how to communicate in an encouraging and healthy way or how to resolve financial conflicts. We didn't recognize that our backgrounds and even how our parents handled money influenced us deeply. We didn't understand that we had *different financial personalities* that were intended by God to balance us instead of frustrate us.

Today, by God's grace, we no longer argue about money. As we have applied what God says about it, we use money to bless and encourage each other. We have traveled from a place of financial bondage with some assets but tons of debt, little savings, and no generosity, to a place of true financial freedom.

And you can too.

I mean that with all my heart.

Here are the things we will cover to help you get to that place.

1. How to have a healthy marriage
2. How to communicate well with each other
3. What God says about handling money wisely
4. How to deal with marital conflict and crises
5. What both engaged and long-married couples need to know
6. Help for situations from stepfamilies to stay-at-home moms

My best friend as a child was Ricky Smith. Ricky wore glasses, and one day I playfully put them on to tease him. And *wow*—was I surprised! I could suddenly see more clearly than ever before in my life. Only then did I realize that I needed glasses. When I learned what the Bible says about handling money and having a great marriage, it was just like putting on Ricky's glasses. For the first time, I saw clearly that the only way to enjoy a great marriage was to do it God's way.

Let's explore what He says about it.

"They are no longer two, but one."

MATTHEW 19:6

"The most difficult years of marriage are those following the wedding."

ANONYMOUS

2

It's

GOD'S IDEA

I walked into the bank to secure a loan to build a restaurant and . . . there she was.

Long black hair, sky blue eyes . . . beautiful in every way. From that moment—that first moment that I laid eyes on her—my life would never be the same. I knew she was the girl I wanted to marry. Amazingly, she had similar feelings for me! More than thirty-five years later, I am more thankful than ever for Bev and for the marriage God has given us.

Marriage was the first institution God created. The book of Genesis reads: "The Lord God said, 'It is not good for the man [Adam] to be alone. I will make a helper suitable for him. . . . For this reason a man will leave his father and his mother and be united to his wife, and they will become one flesh'" (2:18, 24).

Here's a news flash: *God didn't give you your spouse to frustrate you; He gave you your spouse to bless you and complete you.* He has created each of us with needs that are met by our mate's unique personality. It's clear to me that Bev and I complement each other; my weaknesses are her strengths.

God designed marriage for us to learn to love and serve one another with humility. We can fake who we really are with acquaintances, but our spouses know who we really are.

BECOMING ONE

Let me give you just a little Bible math here: When it comes to marriage, one plus one equals one! Jesus Christ Himself tells us this fundamental truth: "They are no longer two, but one" (Matthew 19:6). This unity is designed for every aspect of a couple's life together: physical, emotional, spiritual, and financial.

God's plan for marriage is fulfilled when two people, without losing their unique personalities and abilities, become one. Just as melting two metals to form a strong alloy, this blending gives the marriage union its unique strength. Independence decreases; interdependence increases. Couples learn to improve this unity over a lifetime as they share more areas of life with each other.

Unfortunately, many people get married with an escape hatch mentality

Marriage is first and foremost a covenant. It is an agreement, a pledge, a promise that *nothing* will be allowed to invalidate the life-long commitment spouses make to each other. The exchanging of the rings signifies that covenant. The marriage vow "for richer or poorer, for better or worse, in sickness and in health" says, "I will love you no matter what." Your vows might have been worded differently, but the intent of the promise is the same.

Do you realize how significant those last seven words are?

I will love you *no matter what.*

As imperfect, stumbling, fumbling, too-often-careless, sinful human beings, no words could be sweeter than those words. That our mate would endure our failures, wrongheadedness, and annoying quirks and still pledge to love us and stand by us through it all as we learn and grow together . . . well, it just doesn't get any better than that.

Marital love is to be so deep that in some mysterious way it even mirrors the love Jesus Christ has for the church. "'A man will leave his father and mother and be united to his wife, and the two will become one flesh.' This is a profound mystery—but I am talking about Christ and the church" (Ephesians 5:31–32). The term "covenant" describes the love of Christ for the church, and it also describes marriage.

Unfortunately, many people get married with an escape hatch mentality. If their spouse is no longer attractive enough or finances are too tight, they can bail out of the marriage. We need to slam the hatch shut and give ourselves completely to the marriage God has given us.

Here is what I have discovered about making a lifelong covenant with each other: When both partners are committed to their marriage, they both focus on working things out—even in the most difficult situations.

DIVORCE

God desires married couples to enjoy a lifelong relationship. Jesus Himself said, "They are no longer two, but one. Therefore what God has joined together, let man not separate" (Matthew 19:6).

The Lord emphasizes the importance of the covenant commitment in Malachi 2:14–16: "The Lord is acting as the witness between you and the wife of your youth, because you have broken faith with her, though she is your partner, the wife of your marriage covenant . . . So guard yourself in your spirit, and do not break faith with the wife of your youth. 'I hate divorce,' says the Lord God."

For years Theresa carried a load of guilt and shame. And understandably so. She had divorced her husband simply because she felt he was too cheap and was unwilling to buy the new cars and fund the expensive lifestyle she wanted. Later realizing her tragic mistake, she became depressed and reached out to Bev for help.

"To reach closure and experience healing from divorce, first be reconciled with God. Agree with God that your decision to get a divorce was wrong, and genuinely ask for His forgiveness," Bev told Theresa.

That's where it all has to begin. Before we can truly reconcile with anyone else, we must first reconcile with our Creator and Savior. The Bible says, "If we confess our sins, he is faithful and just and will forgive us our sins and purify us from all unrighteousness" (1 John 1:9). Don't let those words ever become old or routine. What a wonderful and ongoing promise! He wants to forgive you and fill you with His hope for your future.

If you have been through a divorce and you now know that the reasons for the divorce were not biblical, the real questions are, "Can you accept God's unconditional love and forgiveness? And, can you forgive yourself?" God wants your answer to be yes to both questions. If you have been divorced and are now remarried, know that God's will for this marriage is that it be a lifetime covenant.

LEAVE AND CLEAVE

Mike and Yolanda Brown believed their marriage of six years was successful—except for one painful issue. Mike's domineering parents constantly interjected themselves and their strong opinions into the couple's household affairs. Even though this was a major source of stress for Yolanda, Mike was reluctant to confront his parents for fear of losing their financial help. In fact, his parents were using money as a tool to control the young couple.

Mike was placing his parents above his wife, and from God's perspective this is a mistake. Jesus Christ said a man shall "*leave* father and mother, and shall *cleave* to his wife" (Matthew 19:5 KJV). Other translations use "be united to" or "joined to" to convey the idea. When you marry, you are to leave your parents for your spouse in order to become financially, emotionally, and spiritually independent from them. Part of the reason God made it clear we should leave is because it forces us to become more mature and more dependent on each other and our heavenly Father.

Bald eagles spend about two months building a nest for the mother to incubate her eggs. When a baby eagle is born, the parents feed and care for it until it reaches about twelve weeks of age—old enough to fly. Then the mother gently nudges the young eagle out of the nest, forcing it to use its own wings. Like eagles, parents should encourage their married children to transfer their dependence to the Lord and to each other.

This time can be emotional for all concerned. Compare life to a book with a series of chapters that we open and close as we move from one phase to another. Closing some chapters takes courage and wisdom and can be sorrowful.

In this "leaving" chapter, the parents' role changes to that of a coach or advisor. They should allow the young couple to make their own decisions even if they are not the ones the parents would make.

Parents should encourage their married children to transfer their dependence to the Lord and to each other

This doesn't mean that parents cannot offer financial help. Bev and I decided that we would not help our married children increase their lifestyle, but we *would* help them pay off their home mortgages by matching the principle reduction part of their payment. We have also contributed toward their investing.

Children, on the other hand, should continue to honor their parents and seek their counsel without remaining emotionally or financially dependent on them. Husband and wife need to cleave to one another. In this usage the word for "cleave" means to stick very tightly like we might glue two pieces of paper together. You cannot separate them without tearing them both.

Marriage experts Don and Sally Meredith emphasize the importance of this principle: "Every marriage problem stems from either a failure to *leave* or a failure to *cleave*."[1] It can be helpful for couples to create lists describing the good and bad of parental involvement in their marriage. Try to identify everything that might have a bearing on how completely you have made the transition from "their home" to "your home."

LOVE AND RESPECT

Monica and Raymond Chang both had full-time jobs; Monica

earned almost twice as much as Raymond did. She often made spending decisions—and virtually all investing decisions—without discussing them with Raymond, making him feel unimportant. Convinced that Monica no longer respected him, he reacted in a defensive, unloving way.

Their marriage relationship was a classic violation of Ephesians 5:33: "Each one of you [husbands] also must *love* his wife as he loves himself, and the wife must *respect* her husband."

God designed wives to need love and husbands to need respect. For that very reason, He commanded husbands to love their wives unconditionally—no matter what—even when their wives do not follow the command to respect them. And wives must respect their husbands without condition—no matter what—even when their husbands fail to love them. There is no justification for a husband to say, "I will love my wife *after* she respects me," or for the wife to say, "I will respect my husband *after* he loves me."

Author Dr. Emerson Eggerichs observes, "When a husband feels disrespected, he has a natural tendency to react in ways that feel unloving to his wife. When a wife feels unloved, she has a natural tendency to react in ways that feel disrespectful to the husband. Without love, she reacts without respect. Without respect, he reacts without love."[2] Now here is the really good news: When a wife respects her husband in ways that are meaningful to him, it ignites in him the feeling of love for his wife. Her deepest need—to feel loved—is satisfied. And when the husband loves his wife in ways that are meaningful to her, she responds with respect—meeting his greatest need.

Wow. You'd almost think Someone designed us that way, wouldn't you?

MONEY AND MARRIAGE Q&A

Question: My husband loves me and is kindhearted. But sometimes he makes dumb decisions. Do I have to respect him if he's making a bonehead decision?

Answer: Pray daily for God to give your husband wisdom to make prudent financial decisions.

Ask your husband if the two of you can pray together daily, and use these times to seek the Lord and encourage your husband. In a gentle way, discuss decisions you are making as a couple. Then, allow him to make the final decisions for the family. When he senses you respect and trust him, he's likely to make better decisions.

INTENDED FOR A BLESSING

Early in our marriage I focused our spending on what I wanted, without giving much consideration to Bev's desires.

That sounds selfish and immature, you say?

You're right. But that's where I was in life at that time. I didn't understand that Philippians 2:3–4 applied to my marriage: "Do nothing out of selfish ambition or vain conceit, but in humility consider others better than yourselves. Each of you should look not only to your own interests, but also to the interests of others."

As I have grown in my relationship with Christ, however, my mentality has completely changed. The question I now ask is: What can I do with our finances to be a blessing to my wife? Bev asks the same question: How can our spending be a blessing to my husband?

God has called all of us to bless each other, and this certainly applies to the relationship between husbands and wives. "To sum up, all of you be harmonious, sympathetic, brotherly, kindhearted, and humble in spirit; not returning evil for evil or insult for insult, but giving a blessing instead; for you were called for the very purpose that you might inherit a blessing" (1 Peter 3:8–9 NASB).

Decide once and for all *that you are committed to remain married to each other your entire lives*

As you develop the mentality of wanting to bless your mate, you are likely to make a discovery: you actually enjoy buying something for him or her more than for yourself. It's a practical application of what Jesus told us in Acts 20:35: "It is more blessed to give than to receive."

ONCE AND FOR ALL

There is a principle of communication that can be enormously helpful to couples that I call the *once and for all* decisions. These are the foundational decisions a couple can agree upon that do not change no matter what. They simplify communication and decision making and provide significant stability to the marriage.

Let me give two examples. First, Bev and I decided *once and for all* that we are committed to remain married to each other our entire lives. We will never consider divorce or even mention it as a possibility.

Never say never? We *have* said never. And it's one of the most important things we have ever said in our lifetimes.

Second, we determined *once and for all* to always try to be a blessing to the other in the way we spend money.

At the end of each of the remaining chapters, I encourage you and your spouse to make at least one key *once and for all* decision. These decisions will benefit you the rest of your lives.

So why is this important?

Simply because it gives us some areas of security and peace in a turbulent, anxious world. At the best of times, life on Planet Earth is filled with uncertainty, unpredictability, and constantly shifting ground. One popular version of the Bible quotes the apostle James saying, "You don't know the first thing about tomorrow. You're nothing but a wisp of fog, catching a brief bit of sun before disappearing" (James 4:14 MSG).

Our wedding vows, however—those careful, solemn words we spoke in front of God, family, friends, and other witnesses—give us something to hang on to in these all-too-brief, sometimes tumultuous days of our lives. Come what may, I have someone who promised before God to love me, care for me, and stay by my side. And even if God in His wisdom were to take my mate home to heaven, I have the deep, heart-strengthening memory and comfort that there was someone who faithfully stood by me and pledged her life to me.

These *once and for all* decisions have the same effect. Even though we experience many of the unsettling ups and downs and ins and outs of life, there can be at least some areas that are settled . . . *once and for all*. I don't have to worry or wonder about these issues anymore. I can devote my emotional and mental energies in other directions.

That may not seem like a momentous thing right now . . . but when the earth shakes or the storms blow across our landscape (as they inevitably will), it will be good to know that important areas of our lives have been sealed with the power of a promise.

Our once and for all decision(s) _____

_____

_____

_____

Love is patient, love is kind. It does not envy, it does not boast, it is not proud. It is not rude, it is not self-seeking, it is not easily angered, it keeps no record of wrongs. Love does not delight in evil but rejoices with the truth. It always protects, always trusts, always hopes, always perseveres.

1 CORINTHIANS 13:4–7

"Husbands, the question is not, Do I love my wife?
The real question is, Does my wife know *I love her?"*

—ROBERT FRALEY

3

Keeping It
HEALTHY

Ron Perry flew into a rage . . . again.

"Don't you read your Bible?" He pounded the table and yelled at his wife, Connie. "God put the husband—not the wife—in charge. You're supposed to submit to me and do whatever I tell you. I'm the boss! I earn the money, and if I want to buy a new truck, God says I can do it. So keep your nose out of our finances."

Sadly, Ron completely distorted God's role for husbands.

THE HUSBAND'S ROLE

Love your wife

The most important role of the husband is to love his wife. This love is to be characterized by serving and caring. The Bible expresses it this way: "Husbands, love your wives, just as Christ loved the church and gave himself up for her . . . husbands ought to love their wives as their own bodies. He who loves his wife loves himself" (Ephesians 5:25, 28).

God describes the dimensions of this love in 1 Corinthians 13:4–7. "Love is patient, love is kind. It does not envy, it does not boast, it is not proud. It is not rude, it is not self-seeking, it is not easily angered, it keeps no record of wrongs. Love does not delight in evil but rejoices with the truth. It always protects, always trusts, always hopes, always perseveres."

Husbands, I encourage you to assess how well you are loving

your wife by asking yourself if you model God's standard of love:

Am I patient with her?

Am I kind to her?

Am I envious of her?

Am I rude to her?

Am I self-seeking?

Am I easily angered?

Do I keep track of her mistakes?

Do I always protect her?

Do I always trust her?

Do I always hope for the best for her?

Did you fail loving your wife in any of these ways? The depth of love described in 1 Corinthians 13 is *agape* love. *Agape* is the Greek word for unconditional, sacrificial love—and God is its only source.

> *"I never think of occasions like that as a nuisance. To me, they're opportunities to serve."*

My close friend, the late Robert Fraley, used to challenge husbands: "The question is not, Do I love my wife? The real question is, Does my wife *know* I love her?" According to surveys, most wives need to be regularly reminded that their husbands love them. It's not enough for the husband to adopt the old joke, "I told you once on our wedding day fifteen years ago that I love you. If I change my mind, I'll let you know."

No, that won't cut it.

I once attended a three-day conference where many things were said, but I can sum up the most important concept in one sentence: A powerful way to express your love is to simply hug your wife every day, taking the time to look into her eyes and say, "I love you like crazy!" It's especially important on those days when she feels discouraged, depressed, or unlovable.

Genesis 2:22 reveals, "The Lord God made a woman [Eve] . . . and he brought her to the man [Adam]." Why did He bring her to Adam? God wanted Adam to know that He created Eve, and it was God alone who presented her to him as a great gift. Husbands, this is true for you as well. Your wife is a gift to you from a gracious loving God.

When Bev and I were newly married, I met with my neighbor Lyle Nelsen. He said he hadn't gotten much sleep the night before, and when I asked why, he chuckled. "Well, about two a.m. my wife woke me because she wasn't feeling well and wanted something from the all-night pharmacy on the other side of town."

"Bummer," I said.

"No." He smiled. "I never think of occasions like that as a nuisance. To me, they're opportunities to serve."

His sincere comment just stopped me in my tracks. I've remembered those words for years. What an impression it made on me as a young husband. *View requests by your wife as an opportunity to serve her.*

Your authority is delegated

When God calls people together, he assigns a person to lead. In marriage, God chose the husband to be the leader. "The husband is the head of the wife as Christ is the head of the church" (Ephesians 5:23). The husband's position doesn't mean that he is superior to his wife. They simply have different God-given functions, and each is equally valuable.

This can be a sensitive area for couples, especially if a husband has not sacrificially loved and served his wife. She can feel unappreciated and insecure. A husband who has crossed the line from compassion to control can find his wife resisting his leadership.

The husband's leadership style should not be heavy-handed or dictatorial. On the contrary, it should be characterized by understanding and giving honor to his wife. "Husbands, likewise, dwell with them with understanding, giving honor to the wife, as to the weaker vessel, and as being heirs together of the grace of life, that your prayers may not be hindered" (1 Peter 3:7 NKJV).

The husband must obey God and serve as his wife's head by

devoting himself to her above his children, friends, recreation, ministry, or career. He cannot be emotionally absent or passive. He should seek to protect her in difficult situations, such as harassing phone calls from unsympathetic creditors.

THE WIFE'S ROLE

Helper

By God's design, the wife's role is to help her husband. She should assist, encourage, and respect him. "The Lord God said, 'It is not good for the man to be alone. I will make a helper [woman] suitable for him'" (Genesis 2:18).

The classic example of a wife helping her husband is described in Proverbs 31:10–26. "An excellent wife . . . does [her husband] good and not evil all the days of her life . . . She brings her food from afar. She rises also while it is still night and gives food to her household. . . . She considers a field and buys it; from her earnings she plants a vineyard. . . . She extends her hand to the poor . . . . She makes coverings for herself; her clothing is fine linen and purple. Her husband is known in the gates, when he sits among the elders of the land. She makes linen garments and sells them, and supplies belts to the tradesmen . . . " (NASB).

Think about this wife's extraordinary accomplishments. She provided food and clothing to her family. She was an entrepreneur with a thriving clothing business. She was a successful investor in real estate.

What motivates this industrious wife? Proverbs 31:27 reveals, "She watches over the affairs of her household." She wants to help her husband by managing the home and by earning extra money. I love how he and the children honor her: "Her children arise and call her blessed; her husband also, and he praises her: Many women do noble things, but you surpass them all" (Proverbs 31:28, 29).

Her husband's leadership style as head of the house allowed for the full expression of his wife's talents. Husbands, how would you describe your leadership style? Does it encourage your wife to be all she can be within her role as your helper, or are you stifling her God-given talents and creativity?

Wives, are you fulfilling your role of helping your husband? Are you content with your responsibilities and where God has placed you in your marriage?

Submit

The second role of a wife is to submit to her husband's leadership.

> Wives, submit to your husbands, as is fitting in the Lord. *Colossians 3:18*

> Wives, submit to your husbands as to the Lord . . . as the church submits to Christ, so also wives should submit to their husbands in everything. *Ephesians 5:22, 24*

Many think that submission means to become a doormat and never express an opinion or to toe the line and do just what the husband demands, but that is inaccurate. Outstanding marriage author Don Meredith defines submission as "falling in line with your husband in order that oneness can take place." [1] It means respecting your husband enough to follow his leadership.

Now this may be hard to grasp, but God wants wives to respect and submit even if their husbands don't know Jesus Christ as their Savior—or perhaps, know Him but aren't obeying Him.

> Wives . . . be submissive to your husbands so that, if any of them do not believe the word, they may be won over without words by the behavior of their wives. . . . Your beauty . . . should be that of . . . a gentle and quiet spirit, which is of great worth in God's sight. For this is the way the holy women of the past who put their hope in God used to make themselves beautiful. They were submissive to their own husbands, like Sarah, who obeyed Abraham

and called him her master. You are her daughters if you do what is right and do not give way to fear. *1 Peter 3:1–6*

You make deposits in your spouse's trust account by good communication, honesty, and transparency with money

Did you notice the last part of this passage? "You are her daughters if you do what is right and do not give way to fear." It can feel scary if your husband is not handling money God's way. But don't give way to fear; rather, trust in God's love and provision. When you submit to the leadership of your husband, the Lord will work in your husband's life and in the circumstances for ultimate good.

The late Adrian Rogers observed, "It is important to realize every time God says, 'You shall not,' He is simply saying, 'Don't hurt yourself,' and when He says, 'You shall,' He means, 'Help yourself to happiness.' God only wants for us what we would want for ourselves if we were smart enough to want it."

MONEY AND MARRIAGE Q&A

Question: My husband is a control freak. He gives me an amount of money every week that barely covers expenses. He won't tell me anything about our finances—how much he earns and how much debt or savings we have. If something happened to him, I'd have no clue what we have or where the records are kept. How can I get him to share with me?

Answer: First, pray for God to give him a willingness to invite you to fully participate in the finances. Then, develop a budget for the money you're allotted for running the household. Ask him to meet weekly to pray together for God's blessings on the family's finances and to review your spending and teach you how to wisely manage money. A husband often engages his wife in the finances when he sees she is eager to learn and observes her handling money well.

ONE ANOTHERS

The Bible provides a series of principles that I call *the one anothers*. They reveal how to relate best to each other. Although these principles don't apply exclusively to marriage, they do apply to both husband and wife. Bev and I know from personal experience, when couples implement these relational truths, it radically improves their marriage. Read these passages slowly. Substitute your spouse's name in place of the *one anothers,* and consider what would happen if you modeled these.

Do nothing from selfishness or empty conceit, but with humility of mind regard **one another** as more important than yourselves; do not merely look out for your own personal interests, but also for the interests of others. *Philippians 2:3–4 NASB*

Live in harmony with **one another**. *Romans 12:16*

Accept **one another**, then, just as Christ accepted you. *Romans 15:7*

Serve **one another** in love. *Galatians 5:13*

Carry **each other's** burdens, and in this way you will fulfill the law of Christ. *Galatians 6:2*

Be completely humble and gentle; be patient, bearing with **one another** in love. *Ephesians 4:2*

Be kind and compassionate to **one another**, forgiving **each other**, just as in Christ God forgave you. *Ephesians 4:32*

"Submit to **one another**." *Ephesians 5:21*

"Do not lie to **one another**." *Colossians 3:9 NASB*

"Let us consider how we may spur **one another** on toward love and good deeds." *Hebrews 10:24*

"Encourage **one another**." *Hebrews 10:25*

"Above all, love **each other** deeply, because love covers over a multitude of sins." *1 Peter 4:8*

A good way to practice the *one anothers* is to focus on one each week. If your mate is willing, agree to work together at living it out as fully as possible. For example, you might decide to "Be kind and compassionate to one another" (Ephesians 4:32). The world around us can be a very hard and unforgiving place. Bev and I discovered that our home became a sanctuary, a safe place filled with love and encouragement when we simply concentrated on applying these traits.

TRUST ACCOUNT

In addition to living out our roles and the *one anothers*, creating trust is a huge factor in a healthy marriage. You can't have a great marriage without great trust. Each of us has what I call a *trust account*. Just as with a bank account, you can make deposits and withdrawals from your spouse's trust account. You make deposits by good communication, honesty and transparency with money, and seeking to be a blessing to your spouse when making financial decisions. Withdrawals are made by financial dishonesty, lack of disclosure, not seeking your spouse's financial advice, and not wanting money to be a blessing to your mate.

There are no shortcuts to filling your spouse's trust account. Trust must be earned, and if it's violated, it often takes a long time to recover. It's not enough for the offender to confess. True repentance means turning from and changing direction, and it is confirmed only by action—consistent action over a long period of time.

HOW TO CHANGE YOUR SPOUSE

Take this pop quiz. Which method does God use to change behavior in marriage?

1. Your loving, praying for, and seeking to be a blessing to your spouse.
2. Trying to change your spouse through intimidation, manipulation, and unkindness.

We hadn't been married very long before we learned we could not change each other by arguing about money or trying to force each other to handle it differently. We became convinced we could influence each other only by praying and individually growing in our relationship with Christ.

Bev changed me. She truly did. And she did it through her prayers and becoming an example of what it really means to know God.

Although Lake Tahoe covers only 104 square miles, it could flood all of California's 157,000 square miles with 14 inches of water! This is because of its great depth—1,600 feet at its deepest point. Similarly, as we grow deeper in our relationship with Jesus Christ, we can have a broader impact on others, including our mate.

A key to growing closer to God is to spend time in the Bible— read it, study it, and meditate on it. The Bible makes this remarkable claim about itself: "The word of God is living and active and sharper than any two-edged sword, and . . . able to judge the thoughts and intentions of the heart" (Hebrews 4:12 NASB).

The Bible is a living book that communicates God's truth. Second Timothy 3:16–17 (NASB) adds, "All Scripture is inspired by God and profitable for teaching, for reproof, for correction, for training in righteousness; so that the man [and woman] of God may be adequate, equipped for every good work."

There is no substitute for spending time in the Bible, getting to know God, and learning truths about handling money and building a successful marriage.

Our once and for all decision(s) _____

_____

_____

_____

A LOOK BACK ON PART 1:
MARRIAGE: ONCE AND FOR ALL

React: Let's talk about it

1. Have you been successful in leaving your parents and cleaving to your spouse? If not, what changes will you make?
2. Husbands, how can you improve your demonstration of love for your wives? Wives, how can you make progress in showing respect for your husband?
3. Husbands, how can you exercise your leadership in the family more effectively? Wives, what can you do to be a more valuable helper to your husband?
4. Review the *one anothers* on pages 39-40 and select two that you need to improve. How will you do it?
5. Is your spouse's trust account filled? If not, what types of deposits would help fill it?
6. Share your *once and for all* decisions from this section.

Help!—*Online and other resources*

FamilyLife.com
> *FamilyLife Weekend to Remember* conference; and many books and tapes
> *HomeBuilders Couple Studies* (materials for small groups)

2becoming1.com
> Many materials available: couple's book (*Two Becoming One*), workbook, leader's guide, kit, DVD

Focus on the Family: focusonthefamily.com

www.TheGreatMarriageExperience.com with America's family coaches, Dr. Gary and Barb Rosberg

MoneyandMarriage.org: Download a topical summary of the 2,350 verses related to money and possessions.

MoneyandMarriage.org: and check out the Articles section to read more on biblical principles for a healthy marriage.

Free advice is available every day by listening to Crown's radio programs. Find us on your local radio station, listen online 24/7, or podcast the program. To listen or download, go to Moneyand-Marriage.org.

Books:
Eggerichs, Dr. Emerson. *Love & Respect.* Nashville: Thomas Nelson, 2004.

Meredith, Don and Sally Meredith. *2 Becoming One.* Little Rock, Ark.: Christian FamilyLife Publishers, 2003.
Two Becoming One small group study by Don and Sally Meredith.

Rosberg Dr. Gary, and Barbara Rosberg. *6 Secrets to a Lasting Love.* Carol Stream, Ill.: Tyndale, 2006.

Marriage and Children, MoneyLife Basics Series, Crown Financial Ministries.

Encouragement from a couple you should know

Before being introduced to what the Bible says about money and possessions, Hal and Dee Shaw handled their finances separately and amassed a huge amount of debt. As a result, resentment, bitterness, and deception crept into their marriage.

Although they had been Christians more than twenty years, they had not become fully devoted followers of Christ. Instead, they were trying to be "leaders" of Christ, doing things their way and expecting His blessing—as well as His rescue when things fell apart.

After attending a Crown study, they realized that their way of handling money wasn't working. And as they studied the Bible together, they learned that God had a much better plan. With His help and the support of an accountability group, Hal and Dee began implementing God's financial principles.

"Hal and I were finally able to come together in our approach to handling finances," Dee says. "And as we surrendered our will to God's, the transformation began. Yet, the transformation wasn't instantaneous, and it wasn't always easy."

During the next three years, Hal had to close his construction company. The couple sold their home, put all they had in storage, moved in with friends, and started a brand-new career. Then, their son Jason died, Hal suffered a heart attack, and Dee had open-heart surgery. Dee is quick to note, however, that God didn't *take* anything from her and Hal, and they didn't *lose* anything. They already had surrendered the ownership of all their things and their entire lives to Christ.

"No one ever said life change is easy, and I don't know if we're ever really ready to go through the fire of adversity," Hal says. "But this much we learned and are sure of today: God loves us, we can trust Him, His grace is sufficient, He does have a plan, and His timing is perfect."

Dee added that today, she and Hal are healthy, healed, content, and blessed in many ways—not just financially. "We've paid off over $50,000 of debt, but more importantly, we are experiencing the kind of intimate relationship with Christ and each other that God intended. Our contentment doesn't come from the home we have, the cars we drive, the clothes we wear, or even the awesome career God chose for Hal, but rather in the knowledge and awareness of His favor and perfect will at work in our lives."

Hal now works as a financial adviser, and he and Dee have been part of a financial ministry team using Crown's materials at Grace Church in St. Louis. During the past ten years, more than a thousand people at Grace have studied God's financial principles and learned how to be financially faithful as individuals and couples. "Many of them have had life-changing experiences," Hal says. "But whether it's a big change or a small change, any change brought about by God working in your life has to be good change."

part two

The Cheering Section

WHYS AND HOWS

"If the husband and wife were both the same, one of them would be unnecessary!"

–LARRY BURKETT

4

Viva La
DIFFERENCE!

Jonah Williams swept Ellen off her feet by taking her to expensive restaurants and sending her dozens of roses. She was attracted to his live-for-the-moment personality. And as an impulsive and fun-loving guy, Jonah admired Ellen's feet-on-the-ground, more cautious approach to life. Not long after they said, "I do," however, the personality traits that attracted them to each other became a source of major conflict.

Ellen soon realized that Jonah's unrestrained spending and skyrocketing credit card balances were more than they could afford. As she lobbied hard for him to begin living within a budget, her need for financial stability began to make Jonah feel claustrophobic.

You guessed it: Jonah is a spender, and Ellen is a saver.

This is just one of many ways in which wives and husbands usually differ from each other. As Crown's cofounder Larry Burkett used to say in jest, "If the husband and wife were both the same, one of them would be unnecessary!" Your spouse was given to you by God to complete you, not frustrate you.

We all have strengths and we all have weaknesses. These differences can be caused by our gender, backgrounds, personality, and relationship with God. The failure of couples to understand how these differences affect their financial attitudes and management can lead to deep hurt. When husband and wife recognize these differences, however, they can each rely on the other's strengths to compensate for their own weaknesses.

DIFFERENCES IN REAL LIFE

Gender differences

Let's not kid ourselves. A man might never understand his wife's enjoyment of *Antiques Roadshow*, and a woman may not understand her husband's fascination with watching sports on a large flat-screen TV. Husbands and wives are hardwired differently.

And that's a *good* thing.

Although there are exceptions to every generalization, men and women typically differ financially in two basic ways. First, women are generally more security oriented than men. Men tend to be more comfortable taking risks and piling on debt.[1]

Unfortunately, Wade Harrell did not appreciate Patty's need for financial security. Despite her protests, he often gambled all their assets on risky business deals. Wade was so focused on business that he even occasionally forgot to pay the electrical bill until after the power had been disconnected. It was more than Patty could endure, and she ended their marriage.

The second basic difference between men and women is that most husbands feel the burden of providing for the family. They take 1 Timothy 5:8 to heart—"If anyone does not provide for his relatives, and especially for his immediate family, he has denied the faith, and is worse than an unbeliever." Providing is one of the primary ways they express their love to their wives and children.[2] Fulfilling this responsibility is one reason men often work long hours.

Jake Evans worked for the same company for twenty-one years but lost his job when the corporation downsized. He was middle-aged and facing a difficult job market. After twelve months the unemployment checks stopped coming and there was still no job. His wife couldn't understand why he couldn't find work. "Why can't you get a job? You've gone on dozens of interviews without even one job offer. What's wrong with you?"

Her comments wounded Jake to the core. A husband's inability to provide for his family often produces feelings of guilt, shame, and inadequacy. And when a wife complains or expresses doubt in her husband's abilities, he is likely to interpret it as a personal rejection. Wives need to be sensitive not to communicate disrespect when their husbands are working hard to provide.

Early in their marriage, they wisely recognized each other's personalities

Background differences

Bev and I could not have grown up in families that differed more from each other. Bev's modest log home was one of the few in her small, rural community with indoor plumbing! She sewed her own clothes and learned how to maintain the family car. She had to be very careful to stretch every penny, yet her family was generous with those in need. Bev is still an extraordinarily frugal and generous person.

My parents were classic American entrepreneurs. Starting with nothing, they grew a business that provided a comfortable lifestyle. I am clueless about auto repair but understand how to invest wisely.

We were unprepared for the challenges we would encounter early in our marriage because of the way our family histories and their values colored our thinking about money. Our differing expectations toward spending, debt, saving, and giving placed real stress on our relationship.

Fortunately, we discovered that God had designed our childhood circumstances to help us balance each other. Because of Bev, I learned to spend less and be more generous. From me, she learned to stay out of debt and become a better investor.

Discuss your backgrounds with each other and evaluate how you have been influenced by your parents' financial attitudes and values. What influences have been healthy and which ones have not? How can you work together to utilize the positive influences in your marriage?

Personality differences

Greg Neilson was a hard-charging young man highly motivated to build a successful painting business. Deborah was happy being a stay-at-home mom. She focused on the responsibility of rearing their three young children, and she did it very efficiently.

Early in their marriage, the Neilsons wisely recognized each other's personalities. They decided to divide the financial responsibilities to compensate for their weaknesses and accentuate their strengths. Greg built the business while Deborah did the bookkeeping from home and monitored the family budget.

MONEY AND MARRIAGE Q&A

Question: I love my husband. He is a great guy, except that his middle name should be Spender! He simply can't control his spending, and our credit card debt is off the charts. It's killing our marriage. What do you recommend?

Answer: If he recognizes the problem, ask him if you can control the spending plan and provide him with a reasonable weekly allotment he is free to spend in any way he likes. Then, meet together weekly to pray, review the week's income and spending, and celebrate progress. This way he will be fully informed and his spending can be under control. If he doesn't admit the problem and is unwilling to change, focus on continuing to respect him and praying for the Lord to change his heart.

Couples have different financial personalities. Some are savers, some are spenders. Some are careful to budget, and others are impulse spenders. Some are givers and others are hoarders.

Not recognizing your spouse's financial personality usually leads to frustration. It was a major breakthrough when Bev and I discovered ours. Why we acted and responded the way we did suddenly made sense, allowing us to respect each other's differences and reach a middle ground instead of constantly pushing, pulling, and arguing. For the first time we understood how to work together on our finances.

A completely free, online assessment tool is available to help you understand your and your spouse's money personality. (Information is on page 78.) You and your spouse should both take the assessment, which requires only about twenty minutes. Print and compare the results for an eye-opening experience that addresses issues such as your view of money, your shopping tendencies, your financial-management practices, and your inclination to save and give.

Spiritual differences

Spiritual differences need to be addressed if a couple is to truly become financially one. There is often a substantial difference in financial mind-set between one who knows Jesus Christ as Savior and one who does not. And there may be almost as great a difference between two professing believers if one is committed to living in obedience to Christ and the other is indifferent. Only Jesus Christ can unlock the deepest dimensions of marriage intimacy that occur at the spiritual level. I know from experience.

YOU CAN KNOW GOD

We were newly married when I started attending a weekly breakfast with several young businessmen. It wasn't long before I was impressed by their business savvy. But more than that, I was attracted to the quality of their lives. I didn't know what they had, but whatever it was, I wanted it.

These men spoke openly of their faith in God. I grew up going to church, but the religion I saw modeled for me as a youngster meant nothing to me as an adult. I had concluded it was only a fairy tale until a friend described how I could enter into a personal relationship with Jesus Christ. He explained several truths from the Bible I had never understood before.

God desires a close relationship with each of us

The Bible reveals, "God so loved the world, that he gave his one and only Son, that whoever believes in him should not perish but have eternal life" (John 3:16). As wonderful as eternal life is—and it is wonderful—Jesus makes this remarkable statement, "I have come that they might have life, and have it to the full" (John 10:10).

God loves you. He wants you to enjoy a full and purposeful life and marriage, and He knows that this can happen only when you have a personal relationship with Him.

We are separated from God

God is holy—which simply means God is perfect, and He can't have a relationship with anyone who is not perfect. My friend asked if I'd ever sinned—done anything that would disqualify me from perfection. "Many times," I admitted. He explained that every person has sinned, and its consequence is separation from God. "All have sinned and fall short of the glory of God" (Romans 3:23).

An enormous gap separates us from God. Individuals try without success to bridge this gap through their own efforts. Nothing—not education, money, a healthy marriage, or living a good life—can bridge the gap between God and us.

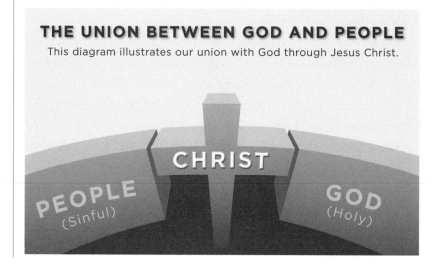

THE UNION BETWEEN GOD AND PEOPLE
This diagram illustrates our union with God through Jesus Christ.

God's only provision to bridge this gap is Jesus Christ

Jesus Christ died on the cross to bridge the gap between God and us. Jesus said, "I am the way and the truth and the life. No one comes to the Father except through me" (John 14:6).

My friend explained that by an act of faith I could receive the free gift of a relationship with God. The transaction appeared unfair to my business mind. Most deals are never consummated unless both sides are convinced they're getting more than they're giving up. But this wasn't the case; I was being offered a relationship with God, and it was a free gift!

For it is by grace you have been saved, through faith—
and this is not from yourselves, it is the gift of God—not
by works, so that no one can boast." *Ephesians 2:8–9*

I had only to ask Jesus Christ to come into my life to be my Savior and Lord. So I did! As my friends will tell you, I am a very practical person: If something doesn't work, I stop doing it quickly. I can tell you from more than thirty-five years of experience that a relationship with the living God *works*. And it is available to you through Jesus Christ. Nothing in life compares with the privilege of knowing Christ personally. It's the only way you can enjoy a truly great marriage. It's the only way you can experience *true financial freedom*.

If you want to know God and are not certain whether you have this relationship, I encourage you to receive Jesus Christ right now. Pray a prayer similar to the one I prayed: "God, I need You. I'm sorry for my sin. I invite Jesus to come into my life as my Savior and Lord and to make me the person You want me to be. Thank You for forgiving my sins and giving me the gift of eternal life."

If you asked Christ into your life, you have made the most important decision anyone could ever make. If your spouse also knows the Savior, you have solved the first of your potential spiritual differences.

If you have accepted Christ as your Savior after reading this chapter, we want to hear from you! Go to MoneyandMarriage.org and tell us about your experience.

ALLOWING THE LORD TO BE YOUR LORD

The second spiritual difference many couples face is when both know Jesus Christ as their Savior, but their commitment to living in obedience to Him is miles apart. Galatians 2:20 has had a great impact on my walk with Christ:

> I have been crucified with Christ and I no longer live, but Christ lives in me. The life I live in the body, I live by faith in the Son of God, who loved me and gave himself for me.

Please read this carefully: *"I have been crucified with Christ and I no longer live, but Christ lives in me."* We are to submit ourselves to Him just as if our egos were completely dead. And when we do, "Christ lives in me." He is free to express Himself through our unique personalities.

If you want to yield your marriage, your finances, and your entire life to God, tell Him so. Ask Him to help you. Submitting to Christ as Lord may be costly to your pride, but the benefits of allowing the Spirit of God free rein in your life are phenomenal. "The fruit of the Spirit is love, joy, peace, patience, kindness, goodness, faithfulness, gentleness and self-control" (Galatians 5:22–23). You can experience a life characterized by these amazing qualities only as you invite Him to be your Lord.

I heartily recommend Andrew Murray's short book titled *Humility*. Its clear explanation of what it means to submit to God is so outstanding that I have read it dozens of times.

Our once and for all decision(s) _____

_____

_____

_____

Everyone should be quick to listen,
slow to speak, and slow to become angry.

JAMES 1:19

"Be a student of your spouse. Learn what makes each other tick
and what makes each other ticked off."

JULIE WHITE, SACRAMENTO, CALIFORNIA, MOTHER OF THE YEAR

5

Communication
WORKS

While I was at work one day I received a text message from my neighbor Carlos Garcia asking to schedule an urgent meeting with him and his wife, Elsa. The next morning we all met over coffee, and they described their predicament.

Carlos explained, "We run into problems whenever we try to discuss money and how we're going to manage it. We both know we've got to get beyond this because of our financial situation, but also for the sake of our marriage."

Carlos had been raised by parents who never discussed money in front of their children. He tended to withdraw and refuse to talk if he sensed conflict.

In contrast, Elsa's parents constantly fought over finances. She reacted angrily and aggressively to problems, especially when Carlos would not discuss their money situation at all.

"I'm so glad you recognize the problem," I responded. "You can't have a great marriage and unity in your finances without developing some great communication. You've heard the saying 'Every household divided against itself will not stand,' haven't you?"

"Sure," Elsa answered. "Abraham Lincoln, right?"

"Actually, Jesus said it first; it's right here in the Bible." I showed them Matthew 12:25. "The key for not being divided is to communicate well with each other and to know what God says about money and marriage. Would you like to explore some principles to help you do that better?"

Carlos and Elsa both nodded.

PRINCIPLES OF COMMUNICATION

"Elsa," I began. "What do you think are the biggest challenges Carlos faces in being able to interact with you?"

Asking questions is a tangible way of demonstrating you care and want to understand what your spouse feels

"There are two areas he could improve on," she said, giving her husband a quick glance. "First, he doesn't listen to me. He tunes me out whenever I want to talk about money, and this frustrates me. And second, he doesn't really tell me what he's thinking."

"Is that right?" I asked Carlos.

He sheepishly nodded his head. "I can see where she gets that idea."

Listening

The biggest step we can take to improve our communication with our spouse is to improve our listening skills. If we want our spouse to freely share with us, we must give undivided attention—and that takes some effort! Maintaining eye contact may be unnerving, and the temptation to jump in while our partner is talking is really hard to resist. So often we don't really listen, but we're thinking of what kind of quick solution we can present as soon as the other person stops talking! Even so, respectful listening is the key to understanding your spouse's feelings and needs.[1]

Elsa and Carlos were listening intently as I talked about these principles.

"When your partner really listens to you," I continued, "you feel cared for and understood. Many couples talk *at* each other about money, but few talk in a way that allows both to safely reveal their true feelings."

I told them that many conflicts result from our mistaken assumptions about what others really mean. We need to be asking as many questions as necessary until we understand the other's viewpoint. Asking questions is also a tangible way of demonstrating you care and want to understand what your spouse feels. And you want to ask patiently, of course, without interrupting. As you're working on your listening skills, you're building a foundation for cooperation in problem solving.

Saying what you mean

"Did you know that some people are afraid to expose their real feelings, even to their spouse?" I asked the Garcias. "Someone might say, 'I don't want to use a budget because they are a hassle,' when what they *really* mean is, 'I'm afraid a budget will stop me from spending what I want.'"

I added that sharing honest feelings enables us to *identify* differences so we can talk through them. Doing so creates the kind of atmosphere it takes to grow a healthier marriage.

"Now, Carlos, we've heard what Elsa feels are the biggest challenges in communicating with you. Now, what are your biggest challenges communicating with Elsa?" I asked.

"Well," he said. "It just seems like she wants to talk about money when I'm exhausted and don't feel like dealing with it."

Picking the right time and place

I had to think that one through for a moment. Then a verse from Scripture came to my mind. "In Ecclesiastes 3 it says, 'There is a time to be silent and a time to speak,'" I said. "Turn off your phones, leave off the TV, and get away from any other distractions. Pick a time when you're not tired or stressed—certainly not just after paying the bills! Be willing to say, 'I agree that this is important, but we need to wait until later to talk about it. Let's do it tomorrow after dinner.' And by the way, make sure you talk in person—don't try to solve conflicts with e-mail or by texting. Neither of these allows you to observe each other's body language and heart, which is a huge part of communication."

Carlos and Elsa both nodded their agreement.

"Anything else, Carlos?" I asked. "Any other challenges you have about communicating with Elsa?"

"Well, this is kind of touchy, but she has the habit of buying things—clothes and other stuff—and hiding them from me. I feel like she's keeping secrets from me and I just can't trust what she'll do with our money."

Honesty

Carlos and Elsa's situation is not uncommon. Unfortunately, nearly 55 percent of couples hide financial assets from each other.[2] Some people think that deceiving their mate over spending or financial decisions is nothing more than a harmless secret, an innocent white lie, but it is deadly to the relationship. I told Elsa that "one of the most damaging things you can do to your marriage is to be dishonest about money."

MONEY AND MARRIAGE Q&A

Question: I have $5,000 in credit card debt that my husband doesn't know about. I'm reluctant to tell him because I'm afraid he'll never trust me again. What should I do?

Answer: I appreciate your desire to become honest with your husband. It is a key for you to experience the authentic closeness the Lord intends.

First, pray that the Lord would prepare him to receive this news well. Second, develop a plan to pay off the debt. Third, meet with him and tell him of your desire to be completely honest. Disclose the debt and the plan to pay it off. Seek forgiveness and ask if he would meet with you every week for a "money date" to review your finances so this will never happen again.

Leaving the baggage

Sometimes our reluctance to talk about finances—or our hesitation to be open and honest about what we're doing with money—comes from patterns in our families as we were growing up. Further, if one or both of you have been previously married, there is a tendency to impose on your new spouse some of the emotional baggage of your former mate. If your previous spouse spent too much or was dishonest with money or was not a good provider—do not presume your new partner will act similarly. Set aside any residue you have from your parents or from a previous marriage. Be careful not to distrust unfairly your new mate because of what happened in an earlier marriage.

Money dates

I suggest that married couples take a weekly money date—it's something you can do at home or wherever you choose. Select an appropriate time during the week to focus on your finances by praying together, reviewing your income and spending for the week, and by celebrating the progress the Lord has enabled you to make.

These weekly money dates are vital because they establish the habit of regular financial conversations *when there is no crisis.* Many couples don't begin a conversation about money unless a problem has surfaced and the panic button has already been punched. Tension can reach the boiling point in a hurry when blame and defensiveness take over. That's when it gets personal and hurtful, with a couple screaming at each other instead of working to resolve the problem.

Prayer

Praying together should be the first thing you do on your money date. Jesus makes this remarkable promise in Matthew 18:19–20: "If two of you on earth agree about anything you ask for, it will be done for you by my Father in heaven. For where two or three come together in my name, there am I with them."

When a couple prays together about their finances, they learn what is important to their mate, and they invite the God of the universe to be personally involved with their earning and spending.

Enjoying humor

There are times when we can become so consumed with problems, especially with finances, that we need to remind ourselves to lighten up. And enjoying the fun things of life and having a sense of humor certainly help us keep focus.

We were on our way to New Zealand flying at 35,000 feet when I broke out in a cold sweat. I put on my glasses to read and suddenly everything became blurred. What besides a brain tumor could affect my vision so quickly?

That night Bev and I met with Crown's New Zealand team and asked them to pray for restoration of my sight. Fortunately, one of them was an optometrist who immediately took me to his office for testing. He discovered the problem—both of the lenses had popped out of my glasses, and I had mistakenly reversed them when I put them back in. I was completely embarrassed. Bev and I laughed ourselves to sleep that night over my blunder.

God's gift of humor enables couples to share real-life incidents as well as private jokes that refresh a marriage. We have repeated some of our stories dozens of times to family and friends and still laugh as heartily as we did the first time. Healthy humor and shared experiences often help couples relieve stress and lighten communication.

Small group participation

One of the best communication builders in a marriage is involvement in a small group that studies and discusses the Bible. Bev and I have led more than fifty Crown life groups, and we never cease to be amazed at how many marriages and family finances can be completely transformed in only ten weeks. The resource section on pages 78-79 has helpful information for you.

Seeking your spouse's counsel

The Bible tells us it is important to seek advice. Proverbs 19:20 says, "Listen to advice and accept instruction, and in the end you will be wise." The first person to consult is your spouse. Frankly, in the beginning of our marriage it was hard for me to seek Bev's counsel in financial matters. After all, she had no formal financial training. But I began to see that her wise advice saved us a great deal of money.

Couples need each other to achieve the proper balance for optimal decision making

Women tend to be gifted with a wonderfully sensitive and intuitive nature that is usually very accurate. Men tend to focus on the facts. Couples need each other to achieve the proper balance for an optimal decision. I believe the Lord honors the wife's role as helper to her husband. Many times the Lord communicates most clearly to the husband through his wife.

Husbands, listen to me. *You need to listen to your wife's counsel.* I committed never to proceed with any sizable financial decision without my wife's agreement, and it has saved our bacon more than once! I recall preparing to make a large investment that Bev didn't feel comfortable with. It later went sour, and we would have lost a large sum of money had I not heeded her advice.

It's important for husbands and wives to agree on financial decisions, because they both will experience the consequences. Even if their choice proves to be disastrous, their agreement protects their relationship by leaving no grounds for an "I told you so" response. When a couple seeks each other's advice, they actually are communicating, "I love you. I respect you. I value your insight."

Sometimes we imagine that buying cards, flowers, or gifts for our spouse "says it all." In fact, it does say a lot. But when we spread the issues of our joint lives together out on the table and genuinely seek each other's perspective and listen to one another . . . that brings the sense of partnership and companionship in marriage to a whole new level. That kind of dialogue says, "We're a team. Whatever we have to face, we'll face together and overcome together."

Consistently asking for advice also keeps your spouse informed of your financial condition, which is important in the event you predecease your spouse or are unable to work. My father suffered a heart attack that incapacitated him for two years. Because he kept my mother informed about his business, she was able to step in and operate it successfully until he recovered.

Setting goals

Setting goals together is indispensable for great communication. I recommend that a couple take a weekend away to enjoy each other and identify their long-term goals. What do they most want to accomplish as individuals and as a couple? Discovering dreams and setting goals help you learn more about your mate and how to prioritize your spending.

For instance, perhaps you are a working wife who wants to have children someday and stay home to raise them. Consider the steps you will need to take. These become your goals. One of your long-term goals would be to make ends meet on just your husband's income. Short-term goals might include paying off debts, increasing savings, perhaps selling a vehicle or even downsizing to more affordable housing.

Effective goal setting begins by identifying long-term goals and then establishing shorter-term goals as intermediate steps. For example, if you know your ten-year goals, it will be easier for you to determine the goals you will need to accomplish this year.

Let me assure you of something that I have seen proven true time after time. The simple act of sitting down together with a pen and paper or a blank Word file and really thinking through your priorities as a couple will be a powerful bonding tool between you and your spouse. You would be stunned to learn how many couples go through their whole lives together without ever looking each other in the eyes and talking about what is most important to them!

May I say one more thing about that? For a husband and wife who are both followers of Jesus Christ, this is a marvelous opportunity to invite the direction and counsel of God's Holy Spirit. James says, "If you want to know what God wants you to do, ask him, and he will gladly tell you, for he is always ready to give a bountiful supply of wisdom to all who ask him; he will not resent it" (James 1:5 TLB).

So as you are gazing at those empty lines on paper, it's a perfect time to pray together and say, "Lord, what do *You* want for us? What are *Your* desires as we seek to set our goals and priorities?"

I love the promises that Jesus made regarding the Holy Spirit in the gospel of John. Just before He went to the cross, Jesus said to a group of bewildered disciples: "I will ask the Father, and he will give you another Counselor to be with you forever—the Spirit of truth. . . . The Counselor, the Holy Spirit whom the Father will send in my name, will teach you all things. . . . He will guide you into all truth" (John 14:16, 26; 16:13).

The key? *Ask* Him! Seek His counsel, His perspective, His guidance. Spread out your lives before Him, and ask Him to guide you into all truth, as He has promised.

As I said, the very process of writing down your goals together is a powerful but often neglected step that helps clarify and prioritize them. The mystery fades as you monitor your progress and make midcourse corrections. Written goals create momentum, helping you both focus on the priorities that will enable you to achieve your purpose. And God will help you to achieve those goals if you have first made sure they are honoring to Him.

Jess and Angela Correll have done some of the best goal setting and planning I have ever seen. Each year they hold a weekend planning retreat to discuss their goals for the coming year. As each one shares, the other asks the question: How can I help you succeed in reaching your goals? Then, they meet for several hours each quarter to review their progress. This has been a powerful tool for them to get to know each other in a deeper way and to keep their spending on track.

Long-term goals

With that in mind, begin by writing down your long-term goals for each of the areas that follow.

Relationship with God:_____
_____

Family and Friends: _____
_____

Service to Others: _____
_____

Career/Skills/Education: _____
_____

Long-term financial goals

Giving: _____
_____

Spending/Lifestyle: _____
_____

Saving and Investing:_____
_____

Debt: _____
_____

Other: _____
_____

This year's goals

Once you have established your long-term goals, work backward and write down what you want to achieve this year. A word of

COMMUNICATION WORKS | 69

caution: Don't be discouraged if you aren't successful in accomplishing all of the goals you've set for a particular year. We rarely reach all of ours. However, when you know your goals, you know what you want to get done. You have a target. With God's help, you will make progress.

Relationship with God: _____

_____

Family and Friends: _____

Service to Others: _____

_____

Career/Skills/Education: _____

This year's financial goals
Giving: _____

Spending/Lifestyle: _____

_____

Saving and Investing: _____

_____

Debt: _____

_____

Other: _____

_____

Our once and for all decision(s) _____

_____

_____

_____

Rejoice in the Lord always; I will say it again: Rejoice!

PHILIPPIANS 4:4

6

Make It a
CELEBRATION!

On paper, Clay and Juanita Diaz were in solid financial shape. The only debt they owed was their home mortgage, and they were on schedule to pay that off in five years. They had three months' living expenses set aside for emergencies and were beginning to save for their retirement.

After twenty-two years of marriage, however, they had developed unhealthy habits whenever they discussed money. Although Clay loved working with his hands in his construction job, Juanita resented it bitterly because he could not earn enough to fund the lifestyle she dreamed of having. Clay was equally frustrated by Juanita's spending, which he felt was out of control. Instead of rejoicing over their financial progress, they focused on what they felt was wrong with one another.

Unfortunately, when couples think about money or discuss it, often they are dealing with problems. It's not fun. Someone is spending too much or not earning enough. Frequently it ends in a heated argument, and the whole experience feels negative.

Married couples will always face financial challenges, but we should balance problem solving by intentionally creating a culture of encouragement, gratitude, and celebration.

BE A CHEERLEADER

One of the most important ways you can bless your spouse is to be an encourager. Let's face it, life can be hard. People can be unkind and circumstances can be difficult. Your spouse may have low self-esteem and not realize that God has gifted them with special talents and abilities.

So, be a cheerleader of your spouse.

That's more than whipped-cream "happy talk" or "positive thinking" . . . that's a true biblical priority. The Bible tells us to "encourage one another daily" (Hebrews 3:13), and "encourage one another and build each other up" (1 Thessalonians 5:11).

Being a cheerleader and an encourager to your mate isn't just a nice thing to do, it's one of the essential nutrients that keeps loving relationships alive and growing!

Ken Jackson grew up in a family that didn't know Christ and where there was little encouragement or love. His father was demanding and absorbed in his work. His mother was aloof and cold. Critical, sarcastic humor was used in their home to constantly humiliate each other. Unfortunately, Ken carried this baggage into his marriage with Meredith.

I met the Jacksons a few years after they had been introduced to Christ as their Savior. Ken had been working hard to repair the damage he had caused earlier to their marriage.

One of the healthiest things you can do for your marriage is to regularly express genuine gratitude to your spouse

Meredith explained, "When your mate is constantly critical of you, it is devastating. When the person who means the most to you is always finding fault and demeaning you, it is incredibly painful and debilitating. I just didn't feel I had anything to contribute to our finances.

"But now that Ken is trying to encourage me, I feel loved and energized to help him improve our finances."

Again, please hear me. This is so important. *Be your spouse's cheerleader, not his critic, not her critic.* Of course it's necessary to work on solving problems—but balance that with genuine encouragement. I was asked what percentage of the time a spouse should confront and what percentage express encouragement. My instinct: for every confrontational thing you say to your spouse—balance that with at least ten sincere expressions of encouragement.

For a moment, think of yourself as a mirror. Do you reflect approval, appreciation, and encouragement to your spouse? Or do you reflect disappointment, criticism, and negativity to your mate?

EXPRESS GRATITUDE

A close cousin to encouragement is *expressing gratitude*. Let these next five words sink in and revolutionize the way you respond to husband or wife: Unexpressed gratitude *feels* like ingratitude!

For example, a woman works hours preparing for the Thanksgiving meal, and her family devours the turkey and trimmings in what seems like ten seconds! Although they are grateful for the meal, they fail to say so. This unexpressed gratitude feels like *ingratitude* to the one who prepared the meal. She feels unappreciated, taken for granted.

One of the healthiest things you can do for your marriage is to regularly express genuine gratitude to your spouse. Thank your mate for working hard to produce an income. Affirm a wise spending decision. Honor generosity.

There are obvious things husbands and wives need to do for each other to make marriage work and run the household smoothly: bring home a good paycheck, keep a clean house, serve good meals, take care of the honey-do lists, share house and yard maintenance, respond to sexual needs, and so on. Yes, yes, yes, we need to faithfully perform all of those tangible, physical things and more besides. But you and I are more than physical beings . . . we are also emotional, spiritual beings. And the needs of our spirit and soul can be just as keen as the needs of our body.

Depriving your mate of encouragement and gratitude is like silent abuse.

A friend of mine described his parents' marriage of over sixty years. In all that time, my friend never once heard his dad compliment or say a word of encouragement or praise or gratitude to his mom, not to mention the words "I love you."

To me, that's almost criminal. Or at the least, very, very sad.

I recommend that married couples ask the Lord to bring to their mind things they should be thankful for in their spouse. In Philippians 4:8, the apostle Paul says it this way: "Whatever is true, whatever is noble, whatever is right, whatever is pure, whatever is lovely, whatever is admirable—if anything is excellent or praiseworthy—think about such things."

Both of you should write down that which you are thankful for concerning your spouse . . . and don't forget to include financial items. And then share them with each other. This can begin to revolutionize your marriage and your finances.

CELEBRATE!

We've learned that celebrating financial progress is hugely important. This may surprise you, but you are much more likely to continue or even accelerate your progress if you celebrate along the way.

Did you know that God isn't a party pooper? The Bible is loaded with examples of celebrating God's goodness for enabling success. The words *celebrate* and *celebrated* are found fifty-two times in the Bible.

This is one example from the Old Testament: "Celebrate the Feast. . . . Be joyful at your Feast. . . . For seven days celebrate the Feast to the Lord your God. . . . For the Lord your God will bless you in all your harvest and in all the work of your hands, and your joy will be complete" (Deuteronomy 16:13–15).

These farmers had worked hard for months planting, cultivating, and harvesting the crops. Now it was time to celebrate God's faithfulness—time to party! In fact, God *commanded* the people to celebrate because He knew it would benefit them.

Celebration is part of our fabric. We celebrate the blessings we have received on Thanksgiving. We celebrate the birth of Christ at Christmas and His resurrection during Easter. Celebration helps us develop a proper attitude of gratitude.

Jason and Debbie Donato did everything they could to handle money the right way. They were generous givers and careful spenders. In the first five years of their marriage, they paid off all their consumer debt and student loans and saved until they had an impressive nest egg.

We should never forget that God plays a key role in our financial lives

Then, the unexpected happened—the perfect storm. Jason's company downsized and he was unemployed for ten long months. Debbie was hospitalized for five weeks after the car she was driving was hit by a speeding drunk driver who carried no insurance. The medical bills plunged them into big-time debt.

It looked as if the only option was to declare bankruptcy and start over—but God showed up. The Donatos prayed. They explained the situation to their doctors and the hospital. And Jason kept knocking on doors to find work. Then, just as suddenly as the storm blindsided them, God delivered them from it. Jason's former company asked him to come back—with a promotion and a raise! More than $100,000 of medical bills were forgiven and the other creditors agreed to a repayment plan the Donatos could live with.

I asked Jason and Debbie to tell me the biggest lesson they had learned through this difficulty. "That's easy," responded Debbie. "We decided at the beginning that we would celebrate even the smallest things that were a blessing. We are convinced that the biggest benefit of celebrating is that it reminds us that God has helped us move forward, and He promises, 'Never will I leave you; never will I forsake you.'"

"That's right," agreed Jason. "We should never forget that God plays a key role in our financial lives. Jesus told us, 'Apart from me you can do nothing.' He is the One who provides us the opportunities and resources that allows us to make progress. And celebrating helps us remember what He's done."

Going through difficulties is an important time to recall previous celebrations of what God has already done for you. Remembering past victories enables you to look forward to a time when you will rejoice again; it keeps you going when you are tempted to quit.

MONEY AND MARRIAGE Q&A

Question: My husband and I both have been divorced and in previous marriages there was constant fighting about money. What can we do to avoid this in our marriage?

Answer: Previously married couples often bring the emotional baggage of problems they experienced. Discuss the issue of frequent arguments and focus like crazy on encouraging each other and creating a culture of celebration in your marriage.

HOW OTHERS HAVE CELEBRATED

One of the keys to celebrating is to pick something you would really like to do or have. Make it a memory; enjoy yourself.

Fortunately, celebration does not have to cost a lot of money. When Bev and I started out, all we could afford was a day visit to the beach nearby. We loved it. No, we couldn't go out to a nice restaurant, and no, we didn't get to stay all night in a five-star resort. But do you know what? In many places throughout our nation, people have no access to a beach. Yet we had a long beach and wide ocean just waiting for us to stroll hand in hand, breathe in that fresh salt air, and praise our Creator for His handiwork and for His care.

The point is, don't allow your budget to dictate how meaningful your celebration can be. A quiet evening alone with your spouse can result in a lifelong memory. Celebrate whenever you can, even the small victories. That's what makes life sweet. That's what makes life worth living.

For example, you may have a half dozen credit cards that are maxed out. Celebrate each time you pay one off.

As you progress financially, you will discover that each new destination enables you to afford to spend a little more on your celebrations.

During the celebration, I suggest doing something that will remind you of your progress. When you pay off a credit card debt, you might print out a copy of your last statement—and burn it. Frame the first dollar you save toward your emergency savings fund. Be creative and have fun! Let your joy become a contagious motivator. See page 78 to read and share celebration ideas with others.

Our daughter, Danielle, and her husband, Kyle, invited a group of friends to join them when they celebrated paying off their home. The centerpiece of the celebration? They burned a copy of their mortgage! Their friends James and Yolanda White attended and were energized at the thought of having a home free and clear. They caught the vision and started adding extra money to their payment each month, accelerating their own debt-free, mortgage-free day—all because a friend asked them to attend a celebration.

I love the way Bev puts it: "Learn to celebrate, celebrate, celebrate! Celebrate your financial victories every week. Concentrate on affirming each other's strengths and praying together for God's direction and favor on your finances."

That is what we have done for years, and we're so glad that we have.

Our once and for all decision(s) _____

_____

_____

_____

A LOOK BACK AT PART 2:

THE CHEERING SECTION: WHYS AND HOWS

React: Let's talk about it

1. How would you describe the biggest differences (personality and background) between you and your spouse? How do these differences affect your marriage?
2. What strengths does your spouse possess that can support your areas of weakness? What strengths do you have that can shore up your spouse's weaknesses?
3. How would you rate your ability to communicate with your spouse? What will you do to improve your communication skills?
4. Describe the major long-term goals that you and your mate have agreed upon. If you have not established long-term goals as a couple, how will you?
5. Do you encourage your spouse and intentionally celebrate financial progress? If so, describe what you do. If not, what will you do to improve?
6. Share your *once and for all* decisions from this section.

Help!—*Online and other resources*

To understand your differences: Crown Financial Ministries has developed an excellent online assessment tool that has helped thousands understand their "Money Personality." *It is completely free.* Log on to MoneyandMarriage.org and take the Crown Money Map Personality I.D. profile.

To help you set goals: For a detailed example of setting goals, log on to www.MoneyandMarriage.org/goals

Visit CrownMoneyMap.org to learn about creative celebration ideas. Then pray about it. Talk about it. And go for it! Later, return to the Web site to tell others about your creative celebrations.

Books

Murray, Andrew. *Humility*. Minneapolis: Bethany House, 2001.

Rosberg, Dr. Gary, and Barbara Rosberg. *Improving Communication in Your Marriage*. Little Rock, Ark.: FamilyLife Publishing, 2000.

Encouragement from a couple you should know

In 2003 Daniela and Chris Jones added to their existing consumer debt and car loan by buying a house. Shortly thereafter they received a letter from a credit card company offering them $2,500 to be deposited in their bank account at 0 percent interest for a year.

The couple accepted the offer, even though Daniela had always tried to avoid credit card debt that she could not pay off by the end of the month. "Due to our financial situation and some needed home repairs, we went ahead with it," she says. Two years later and after several more home repairs, the couple found themselves with $10,000 in credit card debt.

Daniela heard about the Crown Money Map and ordered a copy for herself and Chris. They used a portion of their tax return to help themselves set up the $1,000 emergency fund listed in Destination 1. However, they didn't try to establish a spending plan.

Almost one year later, Daniela was listening to Crown's radio program and heard about the ministry's volunteer Money Map Coaches, but she always seemed too busy to schedule an appointment. Then, on Crown.org she learned that she could chat live with an online coach, who offered to walk her and her husband through the process of setting up a budget.

"With God's help and guidance, using a Money Map coach completely changed our financial situation and our marriage," Daniela says. "We began by keeping a thirty-day diary, and by the end of 2006, we had our budget set up. In January 2007 we began working on paying off our debt and snowballing our payments. We have paid off all of our debt other than the home mortgage."

Also in January 2007, the couple felt God wanted them to adopt a small child from Russia. Looking back, they realize that if they hadn't gotten their financial house in order, they would have missed this adoption opportunity. "We are also in a position to be able to go to the mission field, which is what we feel led to do, and are planning to do," Daniela says. "We have looked at the numbers and calculated that in two years, by selling our business we can pay off our home and leave debt-free!"

Daniela says they are delighted to see their eight-year-old son interested in what she and Chris are doing financially. Their four-year-old son is not yet old enough to understand, but they are involving both boys. "When we got our credit cards paid off, we told our oldest that we would go to our favorite restaurant and celebrate that following Sunday," Daniela says. "That morning at church he told almost everybody."

Because of her own experience with online coaching, Daniela recommends it to others. And she recently completed the training to become an online coach herself. "I am excited to serve the Lord through Crown," she says.

part three

Money

INS AND OUTS OF INCOME AND OUTGO

Steady plodding brings prosperity.

—PROVERBS 21:5 TLB

7

Your
MONEY MAP

For the first time, Tom and Rita Warren felt as if they had hope. After years of procrastinating, they finally started using a spending plan—a budget—and were able to control their spending and create a monthly surplus. Tom called me on my cell phone, and I could hear his excitement.

"We should have started this years ago, but we just couldn't bring ourselves to budget," said Tom. "So, the bad news is that Rita and I have a lot of debt and practically no savings. We haven't saved anything for our kids' college or for our retirement. But the good news is that we've now got a surplus of $500 a month. What should we do now?"

This is one of the most common questions I receive, and it's the reason that we created the Crown Money Map. The Money Map is the journey Bev and I have been on for more than thirty years. As I mentioned before, when we started our journey, we had some assets but were on the hook for a mountain of debt, had little cash in the bank, and we weren't generous givers.

Once we learned God's way of handling money, we wanted to work toward true financial freedom. In other words, we wanted to get completely out of debt and be in a position where we didn't even need to earn a salary to meet our income needs. We wanted to be able to volunteer part or all of our time to serve our church or a ministry without having to receive a wage.

As great as that goal sounded, it seemed totally unrealistic, and we had all kinds of questions. Where should we start? What should we do next? How could we stay motivated for so long? Were we just dreaming?

We also knew this would take a *loooooong* time and require a lot of effort, but that by God's grace it was possible. Bev and I were tremendously encouraged when we stumbled across the "steady plodding" principle. In *The Living Bible,* Proverbs 21:5 says, "Steady plodding brings prosperity." Picture a person filling a large barrel one handful at a time. Little by little the barrel is filled to overflowing.

We realized this was the way we could reach true financial freedom. But we needed to have a plan with a series of small, achievable steps along the way. And we always needed to focus on accomplishing the next step on the journey no matter what challenges we faced. We lived what has become the Money Map.

Maybe you've used a road atlas to help you plot a trip from Denver to Albuquerque. Or perhaps you've gone online to print out a computerized map from Atlanta to Charlotte. One thing I can tell you . . . if you followed the map, it worked! And that is also true of the Money Map. It *will* get you from Point A to Point B. It *will* get you moving and give you accurate steps and milestones as you faithfully follow its directions.

The Money Map is easy to understand and follow, and is a proven, step-by-step guide that works for *everyone,* regardless of your financial situation. You may not reach the final destination, but you can make progress. And I have great news for you: Each destination along the way brings you greater financial freedom, peace, stability, and even joy.

THE JOURNEY TO TRUE FINANCIAL FREEDOM

The Money Map answers the two big questions—financially where am I, and what do I do next? The first step is to find out where you are.

Find your destination.

Look at the Money Map on the next page. There are seven destinations on the journey. Take a few minutes and review each destination. Check off the boxes that you've already accomplished.

When I met Jon and Mia Wong, they were using a spending plan, had one month's living expenses set aside for emergencies, and had started contributing to their retirement account. They had already purchased their home, but they had not paid off their credit cards or auto loan. So, here is what they checked off on their Money Map:

- At Destination 1—Checked off the spending plan and save $1,000 for emergencies.
- At Destination 2—Checked off save one month's living expenses for emergencies.
- At Destination 4—Checked off saving for retirement.
- At Destination 5—Checked off the home purchase box.

After you have reviewed the seven destinations and checked off the boxes you have already completed, you know where you are on your journey. The next step is to determine what to do next.

What to do next

The next step is to focus on accomplishing the *first destination you have not yet finished.* For Jon and Mia Wong, that meant starting at Destination 2, working to pay off all their credit card debt. As soon as they are able to wipe out their plastic, they will have finished Destination 2 and will start working on Destination 3—savings three months' living expenses and paying off their car debt.

Now, here's what's really great. Once the Wongs pay off their credit cards, their monthly surplus will be increased by the amount they were paying on the cards. If they were paying $200 a month in payments—that money is now *added* to their surplus and can be used to reach Destination 3 more quickly!

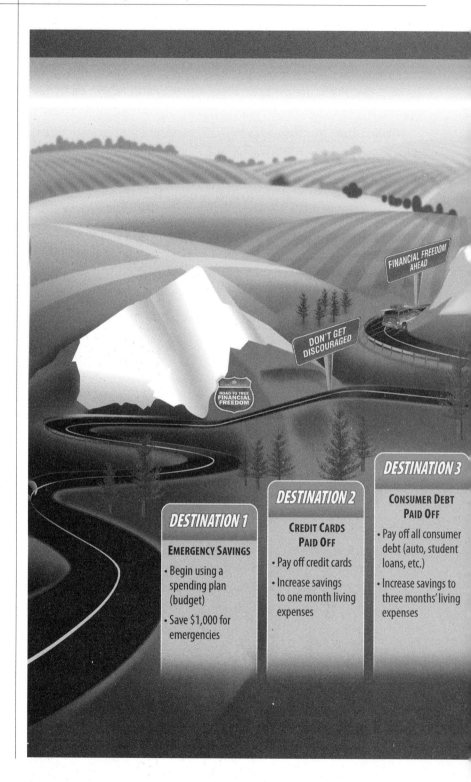

DON'T QUIT
STAY FOCUSED
NOW

TRUE FINANCIAL FREEDOM

DESTINATION 4

SAVE FOR MAJOR PURCHASES

- Begin saving for major purchases (home, auto, etc.)
- Begin saving for retirement
- Begin saving for children's education
- If you want to start your own business, begin saving

DESTINATION 5

BUY HOME AND BEGIN INVESTING

- Buy affordable home
- Begin prepaying home mortgage
- Begin investing wisely

DESTINATION 6

HOME MORTGAGE PAID OFF

- Home mortgage paid off
- Children's education funded
- Confirm estate plan is in order

FINAL DESTINATION

- My retirement is funded
- I am free to be more generous with my time and money

CROWN FINANCIAL MINISTRIES

MONEY MAP

Can you see that every time you reach a new destination, you are financially healthier? You are in a position to make faster and faster progress on your journey.

How to decide what to do first

Once the Wongs start on Destination 3, they will be paying off their auto loan and increasing their emergency savings. Here's the best way to do it. Add half of the monthly surplus to the emergency savings and use the other half to prepay the car debt. Once you've accumulated three months of living expenses for emergencies, stop adding to the savings and apply the entire surplus to pay off the car. If you pay off the auto first, add the entire monthly surplus to the emergency savings.

MONEY AND MARRIAGE Q&A

Question: My wife and I are confused. We are working toward Destination 2, specifically, paying off our credit cards. Should I discontinue contributing to my retirement account until we reach Destination 4?

Answer: Continue contributing to your retirement account up to the amount your employer matches because it is free money! But continue contributing only if, and it is a *big IF,* you can still make steady progress on the Money Map.

For example, if your employer matches up to 3 percent of your income, contribute 3 percent of your income to retirement. However, if you can't make consistent progress, temporarily stop your retirement contributions until you reach Destination 4.

TIPS FOR THE JOURNEY

Follow the Map

Complete each destination *in order* before proceeding to the next. Doing this will allow you to focus, make steady progress, and build a solid financial foundation.

Remember the example I mentioned about using a road atlas to get you from Denver to Albuquerque? Here's the bottom line: If you're going to take the most reliable, direct route, you will first have to go through Colorado Springs, then Pueblo, and then Santa Fe, before you roll into Albuquerque. When you drive into Colorado Springs, you will not be at your destination, but you will be taking a necessary step, and you will be closer! (Besides that, Colorado Springs is a terrific city and a delightful intermediate destination as you head for your ultimate destination.)

> *As with any journey, there will be bumps in the road, detours, unexpected setbacks, and decisions to make*

In the same way, as you are following the Money Map, you will have the sense of movement and progress, with your desired destination out in front of you, waiting for you.

Watch out for the detours

As with any journey, there will be bumps in the road, detours, unexpected setbacks, and decisions to make. Bev and I experienced our share of them. We once received no income for six months and took a step backward on our journey. But we didn't give up.

Some people will make the trip faster than others. You will reach some of your destinations quickly; other destinations will take much longer. But it's worth the effort and even the sacrifices you'll make. Remember, with God's help, you can make real progress.

Pack your bags

Before you start a long trip, you have to prepare by packing your bags. And before you begin the journey to true financial freedom, you need to prepare by learning God's financial principles. It's the most important part of the entire journey.

When you want to build a home, you need to lay a good foundation because the entire home will rest on it. In the next three chapters, we will look at what God says about money; it is the foundation on which to build your finances and strengthen your marriage.

Our once and for all decision(s) _____

_____

_____

_____

Debt is bad, saving is good, giving is fun,
and stuff is meaningless.

—ANGELA CORRELL, author

8

Yes, God Cares about—
MONEY!

When my former business partner, Jim Seneff, asked me to join him in a study of the Bible to find out what God said about handling money—I have to admit it—I was clueless! I had no idea that the Bible said so much about money or that it was important to God. And I had no inkling that learning what He said about it was going to radically change my life and my marriage—all for the better.

As I said in an earlier chapter, we were astonished to discover that the Bible contains over 2,350 verses dealing with how to handle money and possessions. God said so much about it for two reasons.

The first I discovered by accident. Every time I applied one of the financial truths from the Bible, I noticed that it also improved my relationship with Jesus Christ; I grew closer to Him.

That was such a revelation to me! This was something more than dollars and cents and decimal points. It had direct application to my daily walk with my Lord and Savior.

Jesus told a parable that illustrates this dynamic. A master entrusted some money to three of his servants and then went on a trip. When he returned, he told the two servants who handled the money wisely, "Well done, good and faithful slave; you were faithful with a few things, I will put you in charge of many things; enter into the joy of your master" (Matthew 25:21 NASB).

Did you notice the last part of that verse? It says, "enter into the joy of your master." I hadn't realized—it had never ever occurred to me—that how I handled money could have a significant impact on the intimacy of my relationship with Christ. If I handled it His way, it would help me know the Lord better. If I didn't, it would damage our relationship. And there is nothing on this planet that is more important than knowing Him well and experiencing His joy.

The second reason God says so much about money is that He wants to equip us to be smart with our money. He realizes that all of us will face challenges with money, and because He loves us so deeply, He wants to equip us to manage it well.

WHO'S IN CHARGE AROUND HERE?

The Bible reveals a clear division of responsibilities in the handling of money. Simply put, God has certain responsibilities and has given others to us. Much of the frustration we experience in our finances comes from not realizing which responsibilities are ours and which are not.

God's responsibilities

The Lord's primary responsibility is that *He owns all your stuff!* He created and owns everything. That's basic! If you can't accept that premise, then you won't be traveling very far along the Money Map. In fact, you'll be stalled for the rest of your life. Psalm 24:1 says, "The earth is the Lord's, and everything in it."

Ralph and Wendy Gray participated in a Crown life group with Bev and me. I will never forget the look on their faces when they realized that God was the owner of all they had. "You mean that Wendy and I don't own *anything?*" Ralph asked. "The home, the car, the savings—none of it's ours; it's all the Lord's?" He shook his head, trying to wrap his mind around the concept.

"We've always thought as long as we give a tithe—you know, give 10 percent—of our income, we can spend the other 90 percent any way we want," Wendy added. "But if God is the owner of everything, that means we need to handle it all in a way that pleases Him. Why didn't we understand something as basic as this?"

"Well, it's easy to believe intellectually that God owns all we have yet still live as if this were not true," I responded. "Think about it. Everyone around us—our neighbors, the media, even the law—say that we own our possessions. But the Bible reveals the truth—God is the owner."

Our responsibilities

Ralph leaned forward in his chair. "Okay," he said. "If God owns everything we'll ever have, what's left for us to do? What are our responsibilities?"

"I'm glad you asked," I told him, smiling. "The word in the Bible that best describes our role is *steward*. Now, a steward is simply a manager of someone else's stuff. We are to be the managers of whatever the Lord gives us. And 1 Corinthians 4:2 (NKJV) tells us: 'It is required in stewards that one be found faithful.'"

"I'm still a bit confused," Wendy admitted. "I think I understand the part about being a manager of what God gives us. What I don't understand is how we can be faithful if we don't know exactly what to do."

God wants us to be faithful regardless of how much we have

"Great question, Wendy," I replied. "Think about it this way. Imagine that you and Ralph buy a complicated piece of machinery. How would you learn how to operate it?"

"That's easy," answered Wendy with a grin. She glanced at Ralph. "*I'd* study the manufacturer's operating manual."

"Oh . . . and Ralph? What would he do?"

"Trial and error! Totally. He'd just plunge right in and try to figure it out on his own."

Ralph smiled. "She's right. I'm not big on reading the instructions. But I think I know where you're headed. We need to examine the Creator's handbook—the Bible—to determine how He wants us to handle His possessions."

Ralph was right. There are two things about being a faithful manager that are important to understand.

BE FAITHFUL WHETHER YOU HAVE A LOT OR A LITTLE

God wants us to be faithful regardless of how much we have. In fact, Jesus said, "He who is faithful in a very little thing is faithful also in much" (Luke 16:10 NASB). If you are faithful with small financial matters, God knows that He can trust you with more resources. Missionary statesman Hudson Taylor said it this way, "Small things are small things, but *faithfulness* with a small thing is a big thing."

Some people become frustrated by the inability to solve their financial problems because it seems impossible. And sometimes it *is* impossible without God's help. Your job is simply to make a genuine effort, no matter how small it may appear, and then leave the results to God. I love what the Lord said in Proverbs 21:5: "The plans of the diligent lead to profit," and in another version, "Steady plodding brings prosperity" (TLB).

Isn't that great? Isn't that just like our God? The secret is diligence, and moving ahead step-by-step, even if at first it seems like you're taking small steps. *Don't be discouraged. Don't give up. Take a step forward in faith, even if it's a baby step.* The fact is, our heavenly Father takes joy over our first tentative steps of faith and obedience every bit as much as a new dad or mom takes joy in their little one's first steps.

Ten leprous men came to Jesus to beg for healing.

As he was going into a village, ten men who had leprosy met him. They stood at a distance and called out in a loud voice, "Jesus, Master, have pity on us!"
When he saw them, he said, "Go, show yourselves to the priests." And as they went, they were cleansed.
Luke 17:12–14

Please take note of that last sentence: "As they went, they were cleansed." In other words, the miracle didn't happen in their lives until they obeyed Jesus, turned on their heels, and headed toward the priest's office, as the Lord had commanded them.

When they were looking at Him, they were still leprous. When they turned, they were still leprous. But as they went, as they set out on their way, the disease disappeared from their bodies and they were healed.

There is something powerful about hearing God's Word, turning around, and taking those first few steps of obedience and faith. As you begin the journey, God is pleased.

The fact is, God is bigger—so astonishingly greater—than *any* financial problem you may be facing. He wants you to invite Him into your financial life. Just be faithful to do what you can—even though it may seem insignificant.

And don't despise the small beginnings.

BE FAITHFUL WITH ONE HUNDRED PERCENT

God wants us to be faithful in handling *all* of our money. Unfortunately, most Christians have been taught how to handle only 10 percent of their income God's way—the area of giving. And although giving is crucial, so is the other 90 percent, which most people have learned to handle from the world's perspective.

Since most people have not been equipped to handle 100 percent of their money God's way, this often leads to bad financial decisions and painful consequences. But here's the good news. We don't have to wonder. We don't have to guess. We don't have to stick a finger into the air to see which way the wind might be blowing. *Everything you need to know about handling money is found in the Bible.*

Think of it this way. Just as your hand has five fingers, if you (1) give some, (2) save some, (3) get out of debt with some, and (4) spend some—(5) you'll always have some!

Let's take a look through the lens of the Bible at these five things you can do with your income.

"Give Some"

Mary Menendez was weeping.

"I don't want to disobey the Lord by not giving," she said, tears rolling down her cheeks. "But this has been an area of contention our entire marriage."

"I know Mary wants to give," Jose told me, "but we don't earn enough to give as much as she wants. I mean, finances are tight already; I just don't see how we can do it."

"Jose," I said, "I completely understand. I really do. I felt the same way before I learned what the Bible taught about giving. At first I would go to almost any length to avoid giving. Then after I learned what God had to say about giving, I began to really want to do it. I still didn't see how we could afford it. But over time, as Bev and I have followed the Lord's instructions, we've gained more and more confidence in God's faithfulness.

"God has designed giving to be an exciting journey that will increase your faith in him. And—I know this may sound radical—but you can feel real joy as you give.

"So, let's examine what the Bible says about our attitude in giving and how much we should give."

MONEY AND MARRIAGE Q&A

Question: My husband doesn't know Jesus Christ as Savior and doesn't want us to give. I am afraid to disobey the Lord. Should I insist that we tithe—give 10 percent—so that we don't miss God's blessing?

Answer: No, if your husband does not want to give, don't force him; rather, cooperate with him. Second Corinthians 8:12 says, "If the willingness is there, the gift is acceptable according to what one has, not according to what he does not have." In other words, if you desire to give, God is pleased even if your husband doesn't allow you.

My suggestion: Ask your husband if you could give a portion of what you could save on the part of the budget for which you are responsible.

Our attitude

Realizing the importance of giving with an attitude of love completely revolutionized my giving. The Bible says, "If I give all my possessions to feed the poor . . . but do not have love, it profits me nothing" (1 Corinthians 13:3 NASB). It's hard to imagine anything more admirable than giving everything to the poor. But if we do it without love, it is of no benefit to us.

For years, I couldn't figure out how to consistently give out of love. Then it dawned on me—the only way is to *give our gifts to the Lord Himself.* Because He is our Creator, our Savior, and our Provider, we can express our gratitude and love by giving to Him. Whenever we give, we should remind ourselves that we are giving our gift to the Lord Himself.

The amount

Let's survey what the Bible says about how much to give. In the Old Testament, giving a tithe—10 percent—was required. The Lord reprimanded His people for not tithing:

> "Will a man rob God? Yet you rob me. But you ask, 'How do we rob you?' [by not giving] tithes and offerings."
> *Malachi 3:8–9*

While the New Testament certainly doesn't reject the concept of the tithe, its emphasis is on the heart of the one who gives, calling for generous, even sacrificial giving.

What I like about the tithe is that it's systematic, and the amount is easy to compute. But there is a danger in holding to that simple formula. The danger is telling ourselves that once we have committed that 10 percent, we've fulfilled all of our responsibilities to give. For many, the tithe should be the *beginning* of their giving, not its limit.

How much should we give? I am convinced that we should give a tithe as a minimum, and then give over and above the tithe as God prospers or directs us.

People ask Bev and me if we give only through our church. In our case, the answer is no. We do give a minimum of 10 percent of our regular income through our church, because this is a tangible expression of our commitment to that fellowship. But we also give to others who are helping us grow spiritually. As Paul put it, "The one who is taught the word is to share all good things with the one who teaches him" (Galatians 6:6 NASB).

"SAVE SOME"

Rick and Donna Woods attended a Crown Journey to True Financial Freedom seminar. After the seminar, they asked if we could talk privately. They had been married sixteen years, and both of them worked earning good incomes. But they had a problem that concerned them as they looked to the future—they had not been able to save.

Rick was embarrassed as he shared, "I'm an accountant and should know better. But we are completely dependent on our next paychecks to stay afloat. Both of us are spenders, not savers. We're not getting any younger and realize that unless we turn this around, we're never going to have any money set aside for retirement—or even for emergencies. We need help."

You may not be in a position to save a lot right now, but begin the habit even if it is only a few dollars a week

Unfortunately, like the Woods, most people are not consistent savers. Look at the graph. It's shocking! Americans saved an average of just 7.3 percent of their income in 1992. By 2008, their rate of saving had fallen to just 1.1 percent, the lowest savings rate in decades! The lack of savings has amplified the problems many couples are facing in the credit crisis.

The Bible encourages us to save: "In the house of the wise are stores of choice food and oil, but a foolish man devours all he has" (Proverbs 21:20). God commends the ant for saving. "Four things on earth are small, yet they are extremely wise: ants are

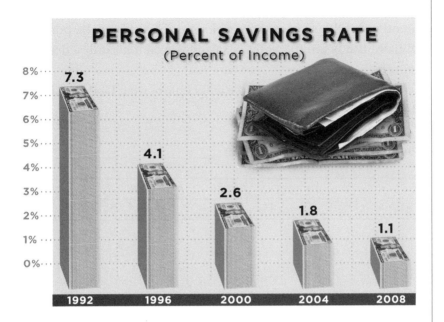

PERSONAL SAVINGS RATE
(Percent of Income)

Year	Rate
1992	7.3
1996	4.1
2000	2.6
2004	1.8
2008	1.1

creatures of little strength, yet they store up their food in the summer" (Proverbs 30:24–25). We need to think like ants! Even though they are small, they save. You may not be in a position to save a lot right now, but begin the habit even if it is only a few dollars a week.

Joseph saved during "seven years of great abundance" (Genesis 41:29) in order to survive during "seven years of famine" (Genesis 41:30). That's what savings is all about: not spending today so that you will have something to spend in the future. Most people are poor savers because they don't see the value in practicing self-denial. Our culture screams that we deserve to get what we want, when we want it—and usually that's right now!

The most effective way to save is to make it automatic. When you receive income, the first check you write should be a gift to the Lord, and the second check should go to savings. An automatic payroll deduction is even a better way to save. Some people save their tax refunds or bonuses. Remember this: if you save *immediately*, you'll save more.

The Bible doesn't teach an amount to be saved. We recommend saving 10 percent of your income. This may not be possible initially. But begin the habit of saving—even if it's only a dollar a month.

In the next two chapters, we will explore what God says about debt and spending.

Our once and for all decision(s) _____

_____

_____

_____

The borrower is servant to the lender.

PROVERBS 22:7

*"If you think nobody cares if you're alive,
try missing a couple of car payments."*

—EARL WILSON

9

Act Your
OWN WAGE

One of the biggest causes of financial tension and conflict in a marriage is—debt. "I didn't realize how much stress we were under until we paid off our last debt," confided Richard Harris. "Then Melissa and I walked to the mailbox and experienced a sense of freedom we hadn't felt in years. We knew we weren't going to receive any more nasty late payment letters. We felt relief, because debt had strained our relationship almost to the breaking point."

God realizes that debt can damage a marriage and His view of it is clear. Romans 13:8 says, "Let no debt remain outstanding," or, "Owe nothing to anyone" (NASB). In Proverbs 22:7, we learn one of the reasons why God speaks so strongly against debt: "The borrower is servant to the lender."

When you go in debt, you place yourself in bondage to the lender. The deeper in debt you go, the more the bondage. Slavery to debt is not what your heavenly Father wants for your marriage.

Now, you may be thinking to yourself you're too far in debt to ever recover. That's simply not true. No matter what your situation, God wants you to be free, and He has provided a road map for you to follow. So let's take a look at how to deal with creditors and how to pay off the most common types of debts.

DEALING WITH CREDITORS

Many couples who get deeply into debt seek to avoid their creditors. But that's not a wise idea. Most creditors want to hear from you, and are often willing to work out some arrangement for you to repay. *But it's almost impossible to negotiate with a creditor you have ignored.* Silence is deadly.

Not to make the situation too dramatic, but hiding from creditors makes about as much sense as avoiding your doctor if you suspect you're ill. Hiding from the truth makes no sense at all! In fact, it is best to run *toward* your creditors, not away from them. As hard and embarrassing as it may be, always take the initiative in keeping your lenders informed.

There are three simple rules to follow when dealing with creditors:

1. Start communicating with them. You make the call, instead of waiting for them to contact you.
2. Offer lenders a written copy of your budget, a list of your debts, and your repayment plan.
3. Always be completely honest with your creditors.

How to handle a harassing creditor

Fred and Marie Bailey had two debts that had been turned over to collections. As happens too often, the collection agency became abusive. They called Marie almost every day at work and intimidated her by threatening to garnish her wages unless she paid up. Marie was an emotional wreck.

Husbands, you need to take the leadership in dealing with creditors and protect your wives. Read 1 Peter 3:7: "Husbands . . . be considerate as you live with your wives, and treat them with respect as the weaker partner . . . so that nothing will hinder your prayers." When Peter says the wife is a weaker partner, I believe he is saying that she is more emotionally sensitive. Generally, the husband is better suited to bear the burden of an unkind creditor.

Fortunately, the Fair Debt Collection Practices Act is designed to protect consumers from abusive practices by limiting what a debt collector can do. Collectors are prohibited from harassing, lying to, or threatening you. You can report any problem with a debt collector to the office of your state's attorney general.

PAYING OFF PLASTIC

When the credit card statements arrived, it signaled the beginning of a verbal war between Alex and Nancy Popovich. They carried nine cards between them, had maxed out three of them, and were using cash advances from some of the cards to satisfy the minimum monthly payments on others.

> *The average household with an unpaid balance has more than $9,300 in credit card debt*

The Popoviches are not alone. The average household with an unpaid balance has more than $9,300 in credit card debt.

There has been an explosion in the number of credit cards for only one reason: *The credit card companies make a ton of money charging high interest!* That's why they keep raising your credit card limits; the more you owe, the more interest they receive, and the more likely they can whack you with late fees and over-the-limit penalties. They also know that people spend about one-third more when they use credit cards rather than cash.

Here are some suggestions that Alex and Nancy used for paying off their plastic.

Snowball the plastic

The Popoviches *snowballed* their way out of debt, and here's how they did it. In addition to making the minimum payments on *all* their credit cards, they focused on paying off their smallest balance card first. They were encouraged to see its balance go down and finally to be completely paid.

Then, after the first credit card was paid off, they applied its payment toward the next smallest one. After the second card was paid off, they applied what they were paying on the first and second toward the third smallest. That's the snowball in action!

Once the Popoviches started to snowball their debt, they got excited. They realized that if they sold things they didn't need and applied the money to their credit cards, they would wipe out their plastic debt much quicker. And that is exactly what they did.

So . . . where do you start? List your debts in order with the smallest remaining balance first. Every time you pay off one don't forget to celebrate!

Perform plastic surgery

Alex and Nancy started with nine credit cards. Today they carry two that they pay in full each month. They also opted out of receiving telemarketing calls and credit card offers by mail.

Log on to the Web site of the National Do Not Call Registry at www.ftc.gov/donotcall to stop telemarketers, or phone 1-888-382-1222. To stop junk mail, call 1-(888)-5OPT-OUT. You'll be glad you took that simple step.

Lower the interest rate!

There is a lot of competition among credit card companies for your business. If your company is charging a high interest rate, phone and ask them to drop it. You may have to call several times, but 75 percent of the time, they will lower the rate.

Another alternative is to transfer the balance to a card that charges *less* interest. Before switching to a lower-rate card, confirm that the new card has no transfer fee, no annual fee, and that the interest rate on transferred balances is not higher than the advertised rate. But remember, if you miss a payment or make a payment late, your interest rate will automatically skyrocket in most cases.

PAYING OFF YOUR WHEELS

Seventy percent of all cars are financed, and most people never get out of car debt. "We never thought we could own a car free and clear, so Ed and I never even tried to pay them off," confessed Kelli Smith. "Just when we were ready to pay one off, we'd buy a new one with credit."

"That's true for so many people," I replied. "Fortunately, there's a way to get out of car debt for good."

And the three steps I offered to Kelli in that conversation, I now offer to you:

1. Decide to keep your car at least three years longer than your car loan—and then pay off the loan.

2. After your last payment, keep making the payment, but pay it to *yourself.* Put it into an account that you will use to buy your next car.

3. When you are ready to replace your car, the cash you have saved plus your car's trade-in value should be sufficient to buy a car without credit. It may not be a new car, but a low-mileage used car is a better value anyway.

Upside down

The moment you drive a car off the lot it's worth less than you paid for it. Rapid depreciation is why so many new car buyers are upside down on their auto loans—owing more than the car is worth. Look at the graph to see how quickly cars lose value.

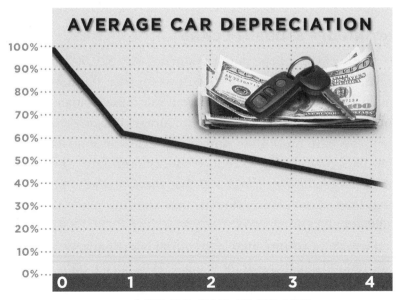

AVERAGE CAR DEPRECIATION

AGE OF CAR IN YEARS

As you can see, the average car loses 40 percent of its value the first year and 60 percent by year four. In other words, a new $28,000 car will lose about $17,000 of value in the first four years you own it. To get the same result, you could toss a $100 bill out the car window once a week!

My advice to Ed and Kelli Smith: Keep your cars as long as they are safe to drive, and buy low-mileage used cars to avoid new car depreciation.

MONEY AND MARRIAGE Q&A

Question: My husband wants to buy a new car every three years even though we have to use lots of debt to do it. How can I show him in black-and-white that we should be buying used cars for cash?

Answer: Most people have car debt all their lives, with monthly payments averaging about $375. Invest that same amount of money from age 21 to 65 earning 10 percent, and it would grow to about $4 million!

PAYING OFF STUDENT LOANS

The average college senior graduates with $20,000 in student loans.[1] Student loans come from two sources: the government and private lenders. The government subsidizes its loans at lower interest rates because it wants to encourage college attendance.

If you have more than one school loan, consolidating them may be a good option to reduce your interest rate. The government has established a Web site that allows you to apply for student loan consolidation directly over the Internet— LoanConsolidation.ed.gov.

However, if you are unable to consolidate, simply use the snowball method of paying off these loans. Make all the monthly minimum payments, and knock out the one with the smallest balance.

After that one is paid off, apply its payment to the one with the second smallest balance, and so forth.

HOME EQUITY LOANS

Home equity loans are simply additional mortgages. They use the equity in your home as the collateral to secure a loan. There are two main ways to tap into your home equity: through a home equity loan (second mortgage) or a home equity line of credit. Lenders have raised their standards since the credit crisis of 2008 so it is more difficult for homeowners to secure home equity loans if they have poor credit scores.

We didn't start prepaying the mortgage until we wiped out all our credit card and consumer debt

Home equity loans are attractive because lenders often charge a lower interest rate. Tax-deductible interest is another carrot lenders use to entice homeowners into using home equity loans.

Don't get a home equity loan without understanding the risks. If you can't pay a credit card bill, for example, the worst-case scenario is that the issuer can take you to court and sue you for recovery. With a home equity loan, however, failure to pay could cost you your home.

HOME EQUITY LINE OF CREDIT

Think of a home equity line of credit (HELOC) as a *giant credit card*. You can borrow whenever you want and as much as you want for whatever you want—up to the credit limit. Your monthly payments are based on the amount you borrow.

The advantages of a HELOC are similar to a home equity loan: lower interest rates, tax-deductible interest, and lower closing costs than with refinancing a mortgage. The major downside to using a HELOC is that it can be a *huge* temptation. Just like a credit card, the tendency is to use it too often, rather than spending carefully. My suggestion: don't borrow using a HELOC—it is just too risky.

HOME MORTGAGE

When Bev and I learned God's financial principles as a young married couple, we became convinced that the Lord wanted us entirely out of debt, even from our home loan. We understood this to be a *really* long-term goal because of the size of our mortgage. But we realized that if we could pay it off, it would free up a big chunk of our income so we could both give more generously and save more aggressively.

We didn't start prepaying the mortgage until we wiped out all our credit card and consumer debt. Then we focused on the home by paying an extra amount each month to reduce the principal more quickly. The longer we did it, the more excited we became. Finally, we also started applying work bonuses and income tax refunds to our mortgage.

Prepaying your mortgage can save you tons of interest. Log on to MoneyandMarriage.org and use the free Accelerated Debt Payoff Calculator to learn how much interest you can save by paying extra toward principal each month.

Once you have decided to pay off your home, let your lender know so they can tell you how to get proper credit for your prepayment.

Some people don't want to prepay the mortgage and decrease the interest payments because interest is one of their biggest tax deductions. But this tax advantage is overrated. If you are in the 25 percent tax bracket, for each $1,000 you pay in home mortgage interest, you save only $250 in taxes—25 percent of the $1,000 interest paid. So while there is a tax benefit, it's not as much as many think. Paying $1,000 to save $250 is not *that* great a deal.

As Bev and I discovered, paying off our home mortgage was a key step on the journey to true financial freedom.

CONSOLIDATING YOUR LOANS

In theory, consolidating a number of higher-interest loans into one lower-interest loan makes sense. Consolidated loans typically offer lower monthly payments, and making just one payment is simpler.

If you have outstanding credit card balances, student loans, auto payments, and mortgages, you may be a candidate for loan consolidation. You have many options from which to choose: taking a personal loan from your bank or credit union, rolling your credit card balances to a low-rate card, or borrowing against the equity in your home.

There is one huge downside in consolidating your loans, however. If you haven't solved the problems that put you into debt in the first place, you'll end up *worse* off. Surveys confirm that about two-thirds of those who borrow against their home equity to pay off plastic run up more credit card debt within two years. So here's the big sticking point: Couples should not consolidate loans until they have changed their habits. Do yourself a favor: Hate debt; start paying it off; spend less than you earn. *Then*, consolidate your loans.

CREDIT REPORTS AND SCORES

Your credit score (FICO score) determines whether you can get credit. And your score may be high enough to get credit but not high enough to get a decent interest rate—whether you're looking for a mortgage, a car loan, or some other type of credit. Without good scores, your application to rent an apartment may be turned down. Your scores can affect your car insurance premiums and even getting a job.

Often, only husbands have credit in their names and therefore wives do not establish good credit. This is a mistake! If a husband dies before his wife, she won't have a solid credit score. Bev and I solved this problem by each securing a credit card in our name that we pay on time and in full every month. When we receive the credit card statements, we meet to review them so our communication remains intact.

A credit score is a number designed to help lenders and others measure your likelihood of making payments on time. The FICO score ranges from 300–850, with the average score around 680. Higher scores are better. FICO scores above 700 indicate a good

Everyone should get a copy of their credit report once a year. Review it to make sure there are no mistakes

credit risk, while scores below 600 indicate a poor risk.

A low score can lead to much higher interest rates. For example, if you apply for a thirty-year home mortgage and your credit score is too low, you could pay as much as 3 percent more interest. On a $200,000 mortgage, that 3 percent difference will cost you $400 per month. Over the life of the loan it adds up to $144,000!

The primary things that will harm your credit score are late payments or nonpayments of bills or debts, bankruptcy, foreclosure, repossession, bills or loans sent to collection. To improve your score, the two most important actions you can take are to pay your bills on time and reduce your total debt. Once you start doing this, your score will begin to improve in about three months. Look at the factors affecting your score:

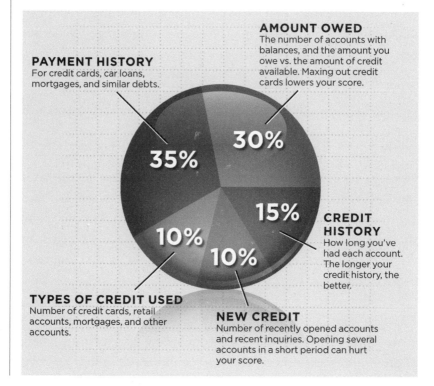

AMOUNT OWED
The number of accounts with balances, and the amount you owe vs. the amount of credit available. Maxing out credit cards lowers your score.

PAYMENT HISTORY
For credit cards, car loans, mortgages, and similar debts.

CREDIT HISTORY
How long you've had each account. The longer your credit history, the better.

TYPES OF CREDIT USED
Number of credit cards, retail accounts, mortgages, and other accounts.

NEW CREDIT
Number of recently opened accounts and recent inquiries. Opening several accounts in a short period can hurt your score.

35% 30% 15% 10% 10%

Late or missed payments, foreclosures, or repossessions remain part of your credit report for seven years. You'll have to wait ten years for a bankruptcy to be removed, and fifteen years for a tax lien. Even though these remain on your credit report, over time they have less impact if you pay your bills on time and reduce your debt.

Credit Report

Everyone should get a copy of their credit report once a year. Review it to make sure there are no mistakes or that you haven't been the victim of identity theft. You can order a free copy of your credit report once every twelve months. To order, log on to AnnualCreditReport.com.

The free copy of your credit report does not contain your credit score. Any of the three main credit agencies will sell you your score.

MONEY AND MARRIAGE Q&A

Question: My wife wants me to cosign for her brother, who filed bankruptcy a couple of years ago. He is trying to start a business. I don't feel good about it. What do you think?

Answer: Don't cosign! A study found that 50 percent of those who cosigned for bank loans ended up making the payments, and 75 percent of cosigners for finance company loans ended up making the payments! If you cosign, you are likely to pay, and that's not all. Your credit will be trashed because lenders normally do not contact you when payments are late. By the time they ask you to pay, it is too late to protect your credit.

COSIGNING

Cosigning is risky business. Anytime you cosign, you become legally responsible for the debt of another. Proverbs 17:18 (NLT) says, "It's poor judgment to guarantee another person's debt or put up security for a friend." The professional lenders have decided the loan is too risky unless they can find someone who has good credit to guarantee it. So, please, *never* cosign a loan.

Parents should not cosign for their children, either. By not cosigning, you model for your children that cosigning should be avoided. Parents often cosign for their children's first car. Bev and I decided not to do this. Instead, we encouraged them to save for its purchase by matching a portion of what they saved.

Our once and for all decision(s) _____

_____

_____

_____

If your outgo exceeds your income, your upkeep will be your downfall.

—ANONYMOUS

I have learned to be content whatever the circumstances.

—PHILIPPIANS 4:11

10

SPENDING

Jason and Melissa Jordan were raised on different ends of the financial spectrum. Melissa's family was affluent, and from the moment she was born her father believed nothing was too good for her. She wore designer clothes, had unlimited use of a credit card, and drove an expensive new car . . . a high school graduation gift from Daddy.

Jason, on the other hand, was raised by a single-parent mom who had to work two jobs to make ends meet, and who shopped at the thrift store. He started working odd jobs when he turned eleven. An athletic scholarship fulfilled his dream to attend college, where he met Melissa.

Jason and Melissa married after graduation, and Jason earned a modest salary as a management trainee. Melissa, however, expected a lifestyle more lavish than Jason could afford. Her frustration with their modest financial situation led her to humiliate him: "All you can earn is chump change . . . and you're the chump!" Their marriage ended after three years.

LIFESTYLE

What a couple spends on their lifestyle can have a massive impact on their finances and relationship. *Differing expectations, if they are not reconciled, can damage or even destroy a marriage.* It is crucial for couples to agree on the lifestyle they sense God wants for them—one that is affordable, enabling them to achieve their long-term goals together.

One of the biggest obstacles to reaching unity in lifestyle comes from the persuasive power of advertising—at the cost of hundreds of billions of dollars *every year*—all targeted at getting us to spend more. Whether the product is cars, clothing, or deodorant, the message is clear: the happy, sexy, wrinkle-free life can be ours if we are willing to buy it.

And if we can't afford it now?

No problem; we can always charge it.

Advertisers are pros at creating discontentment and turning wants into needs.

> *We needed to be content with a sane lifestyle in spite of our "shop 'til you drop" culture*

Five of the six times the word *contentment* appears in the Bible, it involves money. The apostle Paul said, "I have *learned* to be content whatever the circumstances. I know what it is to be in need, and I know what it is to have plenty. I have learned the secret of being content in any and every situation, whether well fed or hungry, whether living in plenty or in want. I can do everything through [Christ] who gives me strength" (Philippians 4:11–13).

Oh, and by the way. Paul wrote those words from prison. In chains.

The fact is, no one is born with the instinct of contentment. As Paul did, it's something we must *learn*. It resists the urge to buy, buy, buy and enables us to live within our means.

Early in our marriage, Bev and I realized that if we were going to reach our long-term goals, we needed to control spending. We needed to be content with a sane lifestyle in spite of our "shop 'til you drop" culture. We decided that short-term sacrifices were unimportant compared to the long-term benefits of arriving at true financial freedom.

So we asked ourselves these questions about each spending category: (1) Can we make lifestyle decisions that will reduce our spending? (2) Do we need this item? (3) If we need it, can we get it less expensively?

I want to challenge you as a couple to ask the same questions about *your* spending and prospective purchases. The objective is to reduce spending so you can create more surplus each month—giving you the ability to give more, pay off debt more quickly, and save more. To aid your thinking, let me share some of our decisions.

First, we elected to stay in our modest starter home instead of moving to a larger one. We lived in the home for twenty-nine years until we moved out of state. We paid off the mortgage as quickly as possible, which eliminated our biggest monthly expense—the house payment. Dream with me: how would you feel if you owned your home free and clear? We came to the same conclusion—it makes an immense difference!

Then, we chose to buy only reliable used cars for cash and drive them until the wheels fell off! Bev drove the same car for seventeen years. We used to call it "Puff" because of the smoke that came from the exhaust pipe whenever she accelerated.

I once bought a truck that cost only a hundred dollars—and it looked it! A sympathetic neighbor borrowed it and brought it back, painted. Suddenly it looked like a two-hundred-dollar truck. While driving the truck one morning, I was enjoying a time of special worship and remembered Psalm 16:11 (NKJV): "In Your presence is fullness of joy."

It didn't matter whether I was driving a hundred-dollar clunker or the most expensive car on the market; I could experience fullness of joy because of my relationship with Jesus Christ. Advertisers have led us to believe that our deepest needs can be satisfied only by purchasing the newest and the best. Nothing could be further from the truth.

It's hard to overestimate the financial impact of driving debt-free cars. As we said before, the average new car payment is $375. If a twenty-one-year-old couple drives debt-free cars and saves $375 a month, earning an average return, they will accumulate about $4 million by age sixty-five! Short-term spending sacrifices translate into enormous long-term benefits.

COMPARISON

Comparing your lifestyle with others often leads to horrible financial decisions. Many couples have suffered by trying to "keep up with the Joneses" whether they could afford it or not. Young couples are especially susceptible, wanting to begin with the same lifestyle their parents took years to build. They often buy homes, cars, and clothing that are just too expensive.

Some want to create an affluent facade to impress others. Don't fall into this trap! Author George Fooshee, who served on the board of Crown for many years, observed, "People buy things they do not need with money they do not have to impress people they do not even like." Someone once said, "Pretense can be expensive."

Jesus taught, "For not even when one has an abundance does his life consist of his possessions" (Luke 12:15 NASB). Think of your possessions simply as tools to help you accomplish what God wants you to do for Him. He has entrusted you with assets that He intends you to use for His purposes—and that doesn't include trying to fake it 'til you make it.

THE SPENDING PLAN

Angela Connor came to me for financial advice. She realized their spending was out of control and wanted to use a budget. "My husband, Paul, has no interest in budgeting because he loves bass fishing," she explained. "About a month ago he bought a new bass boat we can't afford. He's always buying fishing gear instead of the things our family really needs."

"Would he be opposed to your use of a spending plan for the items you're responsible to buy?" I asked.

"No, Paul's not hostile when we talk about budgeting," she replied. "He just doesn't want to bother with it."

Angela's challenge is common. One spouse recognizes the need for a budget; the other does not. If this is your situation, in a kind way ask for permission to start one, committing to do the bookkeeping yourself. Then ask your mate to meet a few minutes each week to review your financial progress. Often your spouse will see the benefit of this approach—particularly if you don't use the weekly meetings as an opportunity to nag.

I don't like to use the "B" word—budget—because so many people think of a budget as a financial straitjacket requiring endless hours of detailed (and tedious!) accounting.

I prefer the term *spending plan* because it pictures what you are actually doing: telling your money where *you* want it to go rather than wondering where it went. It's the best tool to help you manage your money to reach your goals and control impulse spending, get out of debt, save, and give generously.

Regularly review your spending plan because it is a dynamic tool that you will refine over time

When possible, it is best for you to work with your spouse to draw up your initial spending plan. Then the spouse more gifted in keeping records should do the accounting. Meet together once a week to pray, examine your progress, discuss challenges, and make adjustments.

MONEY AND MARRIAGE Q&A

Question: My wife is a compulsive spender. She wastes money on clothes and on her gambling addiction. What should I do?

Answer: Because gambling can destroy your finances, you must do three things that I'll list in order of importance.

1. Love her (this includes praying earnestly for her freedom from gambling).
2. Encourage her to seek professional help for her gambling problem.
3. Take control of the family finances. For her protection and your family's, the amount of money available to her should be limited. Provide her a reasonable budget for clothing and a modest allotment for personal needs, but control the rest of the finances.

These following five steps will help you develop your spending plan.

Step 1: Record your income and spending for thirty days
Keep track of *every* penny you both spend and earn for thirty days to get an accurate picture of your finances. Then record all expenditures under the appropriate spending category—food, housing, clothing, and so on. This prepares you for Step 2.

Step 2: Complete the first draft of your spending plan
Based on what you learned in Step 1, estimate your monthly income and spending in each category of the spending plan on page 129.

Deciding what percentage of your income to allocate for each spending category can be difficult without any outside guidance. Log on to CrownMoneyMap.org to review national averages for successful spending plans.

Step 3: Adjust your spending plan
If you are spending more than your income or if you want to accelerate your journey to true financial freedom, you must increase your income, reduce your expenses, or both. The objective is to create enough surplus in your spending plan to move toward your goals. Reducing spending means changing your lifestyle. This is never easy, but the benefit of ending the month in the black is worth the sacrifice.

Step 4: Select your system
There are four basic spending-plan systems, so choose the one you are most comfortable using. For recommendations, check out MoneyandMarriage.org.
1. *The cash envelope system.* Label an envelope for each spending category. When the paycheck comes, divide the money according to plan and deposit it in the envelopes. When an envelope is empty, it's empty! There is no more money to spend in that category.

2. *Pencil and paper.* Many people prefer using a checkbook and ledger system.
3. *PC-based budgeting software.* Reasonably priced, user-friendly software programs are available to help you manage your personal finances.
4. *Web-based budgeting software.* A growing number of people are using powerful and secure budgeting systems connected to the Internet.

Step 5: Record and review

Record your transactions and then review, review, review! Regularly review your spending plan because it is a dynamic tool that you will refine over time. Your finances are not static. Purchasing a home, changing jobs, paying off debt, and cost-of-living increases will all require modifications in your spending plan.

SUGGESTIONS FOR YOUR SPENDING PLAN

Find a coach

Picture yourself as overweight and out of shape, and yet deeply desiring to make changes. You walk into one of those superbly equipped fitness clubs and find yourself overwhelmed with all the devices and machines. Where do you start? How much do you lift? How far do you run on the treadmill? How can you keep from injuring yourself in the process? What you need is a personal trainer. A coach. Someone who can help get you started and walk with you through the first steps of changing your lifestyle and improving your conditioning.

In the same way, many people discover that it's too difficult to start and sustain a spending plan without help. They need advice, encouragement, and accountability from someone who is using one successfully. We recommend that you ask someone experienced for assistance.

If that first "someone" you speak to turns you down or doesn't work out, keep asking, keep seeking, committing the matter to the Lord in specific prayer.

Think annually

When you evaluate an expense based on what it costs you for the year, it gives you a much better view of its true cost. A Crown Money Map coach was helping one woman start a spending plan and discovered she was spending $1,700 a year drinking Dr. Pepper. When asked if she really liked Dr. Pepper, she responded, "Sure, but not *that* much!"

Give yourselves allowances

One of the smartest things a couple can do is to include personal allowances in the spending plan so both can have an amount to spend as they please. Both husband and wife can enjoy their interests and hobbies as long as the money allotted for these activities holds out. This freedom to spend within boundaries will eliminate many arguments.

SPENDING PLAN

Total Income	_____	**Entertainment/Recreation**	_____
Salary	_____	Eating Out	_____
Interest	_____	Babysitters	_____
Dividends	_____	Activities/Trips	_____
Other Income	_____	Vacation	_____
Less		Pets	_____
Giving/Tithe	_____		
Taxes	_____	**Clothing**	_____
Spendable Income	_____	**Savings**	_____
		Medical	_____
Living Expenses		Doctor	_____
Housing	_____	Dentist	_____
Mortgage/Rent	_____	Prescriptions	_____
Insurance	_____	Other	_____
Property Taxes	_____		
Electricity	_____	**Miscellaneous**	_____
Cable TV	_____	Toiletries/Cosmetics	_____
Gas	_____	Beauty/Barber	_____
Water	_____	Laundry/Cleaning	_____
Sanitation	_____	Allowances	_____
Telephone	_____	Subscriptions	_____
Maintenance	_____	Gifts (not Christmas)	_____
Other	_____	Other	_____
Food	_____	**School/Child Care**	_____
		Tuition	_____
Transportation	_____	Materials	_____
Payments	_____	Transportation	_____
Gas & Oil	_____	Day Care	_____
Insurance	_____		
License/Taxes	_____	**Saving/Investments**	_____
Maint/Repair	_____		
Other	_____	**Living Expenses**	_____
		How the month turns out	
Insurance	_____	Spendable Income	_____
Life	_____	Minus Living Expenses	_____
Health	_____	Monthly Surplus or Deficit	_____
Other	_____		
Debts	_____		
(except auto & house)			

Our once and for all decision(s) _____

_____

_____

_____

A LOOK BACK AT PART 3:
MONEY: INS AND OUTS OF INCOME AND OUTGO

React: Let's talk about it

1. Where are you on the Money Map—what destinations have you completed? Describe how you will make progress on your journey to true financial freedom.
2. What personal challenge(s) do you feel after learning why the Bible says so much about money?
3. Do you consistently recognize that God is the owner of all your possessions? What will you do to help recognize His ownership?
4. If you have credit card debt, a car loan, student debt, or a mortgage, describe how you would feel to have it (them) paid off completely. Explain your plan for paying down your debt.
5. Are you a wise, careful spender? If not, why not, and how will you improve your decision-making process?
6. Share your *once and for all* decisions from the section.

Help!—*Online and other resources*

Get started on your Money Map journey by joining the Money Map online community. Log on to MoneyandMarriage.org , register at the Crown Money Map link as a free member, record your progress and maintain your own personal journey to True Financial Freedom by using the Trip Log.

How does your current spending plan compare to recommended spending plan percentages? Go to MoneyandMarriage.org and use the free Budgetometer to compare.

Start or renew a spending plan by using Crown's online Spending Plan Calculator at MoneyandMarriage.org.

Find creative and smart ways to pay off your debt by using Crown's free collection of online debt calculators. Log on to MoneyandMarriage.org for details.

To help you start a spending plan, work with a volunteer Crown Money Map Coach in person or online. Get connected to one by visiting MoneyandMarriage.org.

Groups/Seminars

Helping you learn what God says about money

Crown Life Group. I've taught more than fifty of these ten-week small group studies. They are a powerful and effective way to learn God's financial principles. One major benefit of the small group is that close relationships are developed among the participants.

Journey to True Financial Freedom seminar. This one-day live seminar sponsored by Crown Financial Ministries is taught around the country. To learn more about this excellent one-day seminar, log on to www.crown.org.

Books:

Blue, Ron. *The New Master Your Money.* Chicago: Moody, 2004.

Burkett, Larry. *Family Financial Workbook: A Family Budgeting Guide.* Chicago: Moody, 2000.

Dayton, Howard. *Free and Clear.* Chicago: Moody, 2006.

Dayton, Howard. *Your Money Counts.* Carol Stream, IL: Tyndale, 1997.

Dayton, Howard. *Your Money Map.* Chicago: Moody, 2006. This practical book describes how to make real progress on the Money Map; the audio version is also available. The audio book's CDs will teach you the Money Map whether you listen at home or in your car. Both versions are available at your local Christian retailer or Crown.org.

Crown Radio

Learn more about what God says about handling money by listening to our nationwide radio programs. Check out Moneyand-Marriage.org to find the stations nearest you, listen online 24/7, or podcast the programs.

Encouragement from a couple you should know

Solomon and Deona entered their marriage with $90,000 in student loans and consumer debts. For the first two years after saying their vows, they struggled to find clarity on the issue of money.

Their debt put a lot of pressure on them to get their financial house in order, but they didn't know how to prioritize their goals. Solomon wanted to follow an all-out strategy of debt reduction. Deona wanted to pay off debt but also wanted to save and invest. And she wanted to scale down their budget so they didn't have to rely on both of their incomes.

After reaching an impasse and concluding that they had no money to pay a financial counselor, the couple began asking God for a solution. Deona called Crown's radio program to ask a question, and in response she received a copy of the Crown Money Map.

They were surprised when the map arrived in the mail, and when they unfolded it, they realized their disagreement over what to do was resolved. The map was their answer to prayer! It charted a course for them and gave them a prioritized checklist that eliminated a lot of their financial debates.

Like most couples, they were able to check off some steps on the map, and they resolved to follow its directions in the years ahead. Solomon, age 35, and Deona, age 34, have now paid off $16,000 of their $90,000 debt. One year from now they hope to have eliminated another $15,000 of what they owe.

The couple is focusing on the higher-interest consumer portion of their total debt, which they hope to have eliminated before starting their family. This will leave only the lower interest student loan portion of the debt after they have transitioned to one income, since Deona plans to stay home with their children.

"Besides paying off over $16,000 in consumer debt so far, one of the biggest benefits has been learning how to create a financial plan, stick to the plan, and make wise decisions about our money along the way," Deona says. "Since seeking biblical guidance, we have become living examples of how following God's financial principles works when you feel like you're drowning in debt and don't know how you will ever get ahead. We are excited to be able to share with family and friends who are currently facing similar challenges."

Deona says she and Solomon are grateful to God for seeing their struggles and leading them to the biblical teaching they needed. Instead of letting them continue feeling bad about where their past decisions had led them, God provided an answer to their prayers. "The Bible is true," Deona says. "Its teachings are relevant to what happens in our lives today. Praise the Lord for loving us so much that He left His Word to guide us through life's difficulties and bring us back to the straight and narrow when we go astray!"

part four

Snags

COMMON PROBLEMS
AND COMPLICATIONS

We also rejoice in our sufferings, because we know that
suffering produces perseverance; perseverance, character;
and character, hope.

—Romans 5:3–4

"If God subtracted one pain, one heartache,
one disappointment from my life, I would be less than
the person I am now, less the person God wants me to be,
and my ministry would be less than He intends."

—Ron Dunn

11

CHALLENGES

There was a knock at the door. We had looked forward to this day for so long. Would he be all we had dreamed?

Bev and I raced for the door. Together we threw it open, and there he was. Tiny, gorgeous, absolutely precious. Four-day-old Andrew, the baby we hoped to adopt, captured our hearts the moment we held him in our arms. We were already in love with him.

Several months later we began to suspect that Andrew might have some physical challenges. The doctors discovered that, tragically, he had been born with only a fraction of his brain, as a result of his birth mother's addiction to powerful narcotics during her pregnancy.

It was a very difficult time for us emotionally, physically, and financially. Andrew became hydrocephalic and required multiple surgeries. Because he suffered constant pain, he required around-the-clock care, which led to Bev's exhaustion and almost complete physical breakdown.

Some challenges build slowly and can be anticipated; others appear without warning. Some are consequences of our own actions; others are completely beyond our control. A job loss, home foreclosure, major illness, birth of a special-needs child, business reversal, death of a family member, identity theft, military deployment of a breadwinner, bankruptcy, or any number of other problems can exert major stress on a marriage and finances. Surveys reveal that many marriages do not survive the stress of these predicaments.

A SOLID FRAMEWORK

You can't prevent every difficulty and you can't dodge every storm, but you can prepare to survive them by building a solid relationship with the Lord, a healthy marriage, and stable finances. The stronger your marriage and the healthier your finances, the better you are able to cope. Proverbs 27:12 says, "The prudent see danger and take refuge, but the simple keep going and suffer for it."

Financial problems can be an incredible drain on our mental, emotional, and spiritual reserves, sapping our ability to respond to those inevitable life challenges that all of us face from time to time.

That's why this simple book you hold in your hands is so important to you, now and in the future. By the time you finish reading, you will know God's framework for marriage and managing money. But knowing is only half of the preparation you need. The other half is applying what you have learned.

Jesus illustrated it this way: "Everyone who hears these words of mine and puts them into practice is like a wise man who built his house on the rock. The rain came down, the streams rose, and the winds blew and beat against that house; yet it did not fall, because it had its foundation on the rock. But everyone who hears these words of mine and does not put them into practice is like a foolish man who built his house on sand. The rain came down, the streams rose, and the winds blew and beat against that house, and it fell with a great crash" (Matthew 7:24–27).

The more time you as a couple spend getting to know God and what He reveals in the Bible—conscientiously applying what you've learned—the better prepared you will be to weather life's storms. And this may surprise you, but God will even orchestrate those storms for your ultimate benefit! Romans 8:28 tells us, "We know that in all things God works for the good of those who love him, who have been called according to his purpose."

Bev and I have endured—and benefited from—many storms. The one surrounding Andrew's birth with most of his brain missing drew us much closer to each other and to the Lord than we had ever been before. Through the crucible of our pain, fatigue, suffering, and tears, many of the Bible's truths grew from wispy theory into rock-solid reality beneath our feet. We began to grasp how deeply God loved and cared for Andrew. And for us. Although we would never want to repeat this experience—or anything close to it—we are incredibly grateful for how the Lord used it in our lives.

Ron Dunn observed: "If God subtracted one pain, one heartache, one disappointment from my life, I would be less than the person I am now, less the person God wants me to be, and my ministry would be less than He intends." What I'm saying here is recognize difficulties as opportunities to grow into the couple God wants you to be.

I know what you're thinking . . . "Easy for you to say, Howard. You have no idea what we've been through." Granted. But then, I could also say, "You have no idea what *we* have been through." And yet Bev and I are here to testify that the Lord Jesus has stood with us in every crisis, every heartache, every difficult decision. Every one of those incidents, painful as they may have been, have brought us closer to Him, and closer to each other.

Romans 5:3–4 tells us, "We also rejoice in our sufferings, because we know that suffering produces perseverance; perseverance, character; and character, hope."

Financial preparation

One of the biggest benefits of making progress on the Crown Money Map, is that it provides financial margin when you have a challenging occasion. By the time Andrew was born, we had paid off all our debts, including the mortgage. Later, when we discovered his physical problems, we knew that his medical expenses would be a challenge even though we were debt-free. And they were, but our freedom from debt enabled us to focus on each other, preserving a strong marriage as we dealt with Andrew's problems.

COMMON CHALLENGES
When challenges come

When a storm surges, your first step is to communicate. Tell the Lord and each other your feelings and concerns. How important is this? It's important enough to schedule a time *every day* to share, so you can encourage each other and maintain a solid marriage.

It is also critical to evaluate quickly how the circumstance will affect your finances and to make the necessary adjustments for any diminished income or increased expenses. If you have children old enough to understand, invite them to participate with you in discussing how the entire family can help make ends meet.

> *Never attempt to go through a storm alone*

Never attempt to go through a storm alone. Seek advice from people who have been through a similar situation. You will draw strength not only from their emotional support but also from their experience. They have gained valuable knowledge: mistakes to avoid and resources to help. Ask your church and friends to pray; it's their most powerful contribution. Let's examine some of the most common financial challenges couples face.

Job loss

A job loss ranks among life's most stressful events—not just for the unemployed but for the spouse, as well. Meet together as soon as possible after the job loss, and discuss ways to minimize the emotional and financial toll on both of you. Then draw up a game plan for the job search—from drafting a résumé to networking with friends. When you lose a job, your full-time job should be finding a new job.

In addition to cutting back on spending for discretionary items, there are two financial goals to keep in mind. Limit the amount of debt used for living expenses. Many couples mask the real situation by using debt to fund their current spending.

Make good, hard decisions not to spend one penny you don't have to. Every borrowed penny must be repaid—and with interest—and although spending it is the easy part, repayment is hard work.

Do what you can to maintain health insurance. You may be able to assume your health insurance coverage through a COBRA plan from your former employer. If not, get advice from others on cost-efficient coverage.

Illness or accident

If one of you suffers a major illness or accident—particularly a working spouse—it's a double whammy. Medical expenses pile up as income plunges. If the condition is severe enough to prevent future employment, you will need to make permanent adjustments. And if either health insurance or disability coverage is inadequate, it can be financially catastrophic.

Be prepared for the possibility of one of you having to make important decisions without the benefit of input from the other. Bev and I have decided that if one of us is seriously ill, the other will make the financial and health-related decisions. We are each familiar with the location of all important records and know how to use them.

Determine the facts as soon as possible and get advice from people you trust. Keep careful track of all medical expenses and don't hesitate to question any suspicious charges.

Don't be reluctant or embarrassed to make your needs known to your family, friends, and church. Pride is a weight too heavy to bear . . . especially in a small boat on a stormy stretch of ocean. When you sail into a tempest, radio for help. Call the Coast Guard. In other words, extend to your family and your church family the opportunity to help meet your needs. Giving to those in need is a big part of what it means to follow Christ. Galatians 6:2 reminds us, "Carry each other's burdens, and in this way you will fulfill the law of Christ."

MONEY AND MARRIAGE Q&A

Question: My wife wants her elderly parents to come live with us, but I think they should go to an assisted-living facility. How can we resolve this issue?

Answer: Pray together daily, asking the Lord to show you both what He wants you to do. If you are reluctant to have them in your home because you can't afford to renovate it or care for them, seek other solutions. For example, if your wife has siblings, ask if they can help.

Boomerangs

Ted and Samantha Brady couldn't believe their ears. "I really want to move back home," pleaded their son Jeremy. He had earned his college degree but hadn't yet found the right job. "As soon as I get on my feet, I'll get my own place," he assured them.

More and more adult children are returning to live with Mom and Dad because of the high cost of living. So many are returning that this group has been called the "boomerang generation." Our son Matt moved back home for a year, and it turned out to be an amazing opportunity to spend time together. We were able to provide advice and encouragement as he started his career.

It's very important, however, to agree upon certain ground rules. How much will she contribute toward room and board? What will he be responsible for in the way of household chores? Although somewhat hidden, there are very real costs involved when an additional adult resides in the home. It will help your adult children mature—and sometimes motivate them to find a job—as they contribute to the family budget.

Repossession, foreclosure, and bankruptcy

Car repossession, losing a home through foreclosure, bankruptcy—all of these are traumatic losses. In the midst of these circumstances it is important for couples to remember to communicate well and pray daily together to preserve and grow their marriage.

Remember, others have faced these same storms and survived. Even though it's stressful, it's not the end of the world. The Lord is fully able to guide you and your spouse through crises such as these, and worse besides.

Each of these situations calls for practical steps to minimize the negative impact.

Repossession: If you find yourself unable to make your car payments, you really have only two options. You can sell the car yourself or have the lender repossess it. Do everything you can to avoid repossession. It may seem easy at the moment to just let the lender take it, but you will pay in the end. Typically it will be sold at auction for much less than you could sell it for yourself. Yet, you remain liable for the deficiency—the difference between what you owe and what it sells for.

> *Remember, others have faced these same storms and survived. Even though it's stressful, it's not the end of the world*

So, if you don't have enough money on hand, try to get a loan for the difference between the sales price and the amount you owe. Then sell the car yourself and pay off the car loan. This requires a little more work, but it has three distinct advantages.

1. You will owe less after the sale by selling it yourself.
2. You protect your credit score.
3. You honor the Lord by not violating your agreement with the creditor.

Foreclosure: If you're in a home you can't afford, talk to your mortgage lender before you miss your first payment. Hiding from your lender at this point makes about as much sense as the proverbial ostrich hiding her head in the sand. The longer you wait to communicate, the fewer options you'll have.

Here's a newsflash: Even in the middle of a housing crisis

lenders usually don't want to foreclose, because it's expensive for them. Often they are open to working with borrowers to avoid it. Here are a few options:

- *Put your home up for sale.* If you are unable to sell it for enough to cover the mortgage, talk to the lender about the possibility of a *deed in lieu of foreclosure* or a *short sale.*
- *Deed in lieu of foreclosure.* The lender agrees to take the deed to your home without going through foreclosure.
- *Short Sale.* If you have no equity in the home, a "short sale" means the lender agrees to accept the proceeds from the sale of your home, even if they don't cover the amount you owe.

For example, suppose a couple owes $100,000 on a home. The bank agrees to accept the $75,000 they sell it for and write off the remaining $25,000 of the original mortgage. The couple is then free of the debt, but walks away with nothing.

A disadvantage of the short sale is that in most cases, the debt forgiven by the lender is considered taxable income, so the couple in the example above may be liable to pay income taxes on the $25,000 of mortgage relief.

And although this approach usually hurts your credit, you might be able to work with your lender to reduce this damage—something that isn't possible with a foreclosure.

Bankruptcy: The Bible never prohibits bankruptcy, but it does discourage it: "The wicked borrow and do not repay, but the righteous give generously" (Psalm 37:21). Make every effort to avoid bankruptcy. Reserve that option as a final, unavoidable resort—when you are in such extreme financial difficulties that there is no alternative, or if your emotional health or marriage is at stake.

Bankruptcy is not the quick fix that some think. It destroys your credit and remains on your credit report for ten years. But that's not the end of it; many job applications ask if you have ever filed for bankruptcy.

Although I discourage bankruptcy, it can provide the opportunity for people to regain their financial stability. If you've declared bankruptcy, don't carry a load of guilt. Learn what the Lord wants to teach you from the experience. And—I hope you're ready for this—even though you may no longer be *legally* obligated to repay the debts, you should try to repay them. That's what God really desires.

Repaying your debts will develop your character and you will be a godly example to your creditors. Interestingly, some of the most successful couples I know in business—and in life—have made the decision to repay debts extinguished by bankruptcy.

Remember, you and your spouse can't avoid every challenge in life—none of us can. But you can prepare to survive them by building a solid relationship with the Lord, a healthy marriage, and stable finances.

Our once and for all decision(s) _____

_____

_____

_____

Do not let any unwholesome talk come out of your mouths,
but only what is helpful for building others up according to
their needs, that it may benefit those who listen.

EPHESIANS 4:29

12

Conflict
RESOLUTION

Money. It's one of the most common areas of conflict for couples. God knew that we'd have conflict and even anger in our marriages. But when we seek to resolve anger, we can keep it from becoming a sin that damages our relationship. Romans 12:18 tell us, "If it is possible, as far as it depends on you, live at peace with everyone."

You might be surprised to learn that conflict isn't always bad. In fact, it can be a tool for strengthening the relationship. Although a thunderstorm can be terrifying, some meteorologists tell us that it helps to clean the air. Lightning produces negatively charged ions, which, I'm told, attach themselves to pollutants that fall to the ground. That's why the air smells so clean after a thunderstorm. The same is true when we deal with conflict in marriage in a healthy way. Even if it is loud and scary, conflict can help to clear the air in our marriage.

When conflict is handled correctly, two people share their hearts with each other in a caring and positive way, trying to listen and be heard while connecting on a deep level. Unfortunately, many couples don't know how to handle conflict well.

Marriage expert Mitch Temple[1] counseled Tim and Chrissy Grant, who were having a hard time dealing with conflict. Tim's job was fighting forest fires, and Chrissy did research for the National Forest Service.

Mitch asked them what was necessary to start a wildfire, and Tim responded, "There needs to be three ingredients: fuel, oxygen, and enough heat to bring the fuel to its flash point. If the fuel, such as wood and grass is very dry, it can ignite quickly and escalate out of control."

"What's the most effective way to fight a forest fire and what part does wind play in the fire spreading?" Mitch probed.

"The key to getting a fire under control," Chrissy replied, "is to remove one of those necessary ingredients—fuel, oxygen, or heat. But when you add high winds, fires can grow like crazy. They can jump fire lines and even from mountaintop to mountaintop, doing tremendous damage."

Unfortunately, Tim and Chrissy had fallen into patterns of dealing with conflict that resembled a forest fire. Chrissy would smolder with anger because Tim avoided talking about their finances. When she could tolerate it no longer, she would reach the flash point and attack Tim verbally. Tim would react in kind.

The more your spouse's trust account is filled, the more your mate is certain of your love.

Their basic problem was unhealthy habits of dealing with financial conflict. They started each conversation with a salvo of stinging accusations and it escalated into very personal attacks. And in the process, they were destroying the very things they wanted most in their marriage—love, mutual respect, and commitment. Their harmful words and actions were like adding high winds to an already roaring forest fire. They had become relational arsonists.

Unhealthy conflict can affect our job performance, physical and mental health, and even our children. James 3:6 warns us, "The tongue also is a fire, a world of evil among the parts of the body. It corrupts the whole person, sets the whole course of his life on fire."

Three factors are essential to convert harmful conflicts to healthy ones:

- goodwill on the part of both spouses,
- a written agreement on how to conduct themselves during conflicts, and
- understanding the importance of forgiveness.

GOODWILL

When conflict comes, loving and wanting the best for each other form the foundation for handling it in a healthy manner. The more your spouse's trust account is filled, the more your mate is certain of your love, the greater the goodwill between the two of you, and the easier it is to work through difficult issues.

Prayerfully review these verses and answer the question: Does this verse accurately describe my attitude toward my spouse and the way I treat my spouse?

Love is patient, love is kind. It does not envy, it does not boast, it is not proud. (1 Corinthians 13:4)

Love is not rude, it is not self-seeking, it is not easily angered, it keeps no record of wrongs. (1 Corinthians 13:5)

Love always protects, always trusts, always hopes, always perseveres. (1 Corinthians 13:7)

Do nothing from selfishness or empty conceit; but with humility of mind regard one another as more important than yourselves; do not merely look out for your own personal interests, but also for the interests of others. (Philippians 2:3–4 NASB).

Be kind to one other, tender-hearted, forgiving each other, just as God through Christ has forgiven you. (Ephesians 4:32 NASB)

And the Lord's servant must not quarrel; instead, he must be kind to everyone, able to teach, not resentful. Those who oppose him, he must gently instruct.
(2 Timothy 2:24–25)

If you are not treating your spouse in these ways, I encourage you to spend time with the Lord asking Him to change your heart and your actions. Be candid with your wife or husband and ask for forgiveness for your actions. As you are faithful to live out these powerful verses, you and your marriage will be transformed.

WRITTEN AGREEMENT

It is crucial for couples to write down agreed-upon ground rules for healthy conflict—*before that conflict erupts.* This agreement should be designed to foster open communication, love and respect for each other, and resolution of a problem.

There are some basic dos and don'ts that are helpful for most couples. Review them before you draft your own agreement.

The "nevers": We will

1. *Never threaten divorce* during conflict, because this will attack the foundation of your relationship, leave scars that take years to heal, and cause your spouse to trust you less. It will only validate any suspicion that you have given up and are not willing to fight for your marriage. Remember that your mate should never be your enemy; rather, your spouse should be your intimate ally. You are not complete without your spouse.

2. *Never confront in public* because it could deeply embarrass

your spouse. This will immediately put your mate on the defensive and can destroy the desire to reconcile.

3. *Never nag.* Nagging is not the way to get your spouse's attention to deal with a problem. Proverbs 19:13 says, "A quarrelsome wife is like a constant dripping." And, I might add—so is a nagging husband!

4. *Never verbally attack.* Lashing out leaves your spouse hurt and defensive and works against resolving conflict. Your goal is reconciliation and healing. Tell your mate your feelings and what the problem is from your point of view. Use "I" statements to share your feelings instead of "you" assertions, which tend to assail your mate. Say something like, "I'm frustrated that the bills didn't get paid on time," instead of "You're always so irresponsible and lazy. You never pay anything on time." When you attack your spouse's character or motives, the discussion morphs from legitimate concern to unwarranted criticism. Never, ever, personally attack.

5. *Never resurrect the past.* Oh, what a temptation this is! I once heard a marriage expert refer to this phenomenon as "harpoons on the wall." It's as though we mount our past grievances on the walls of our home—those incidents when our spouse was guilty-as-guilty-as-can-be of sin, carelessness, absentmindedness, or some doozey of a mistake. Then, when we get into some disagreement, the temptation is to reach up on the wall and haul down one of those old harpoons— "Remember the time when you . . . ?" And we let that rusty old thing fly through the air, giving it the new life it never deserved!

Leave those barnacled, obsolete, old harpoons on the wall. Or better still, haul them to the dump and get rid of them forever. When a disagreement is over and there is a satisfactory conclusion, it's over. Don't rehash old arguments—forget them! In other words, don't get *historical* in your marriage by continually bringing up the past. First Corinthians 13:5 (NASB) tells us, "Love does not take into account a wrong suffered."

"Always": Instead, we will

1. *Always ask permission to address the conflict.* Make sure your mate is ready to face the issue before you discuss it. Asking permission with kindness helps sets the stage for resolution.

2. *Always invite God to be part of your discussion.* When you start your time together by praying, it can completely change the tone of your conversation. And if you can't seem to find the answers to your problems, pray again. James 1:5 says, "If any of you lacks wisdom, he should ask God, who gives generously to all without finding fault, and it will be given to him." Nothing will cool a heated confrontation more quickly than the words, "Let's pray!"

3. *Always admit when you're wrong.* Sometimes a conflict occurs because one person's behavior was inappropriate. Be willing to confess and ask forgiveness if you've done something wrong so you can help heal the damage to your relationship. Try something like, "I'm so sorry I was unkind to you. Will you please forgive me?"

4. *Always listen.* Seek to understand where your mate is coming from, even when you may not agree with his or her viewpoint. Learn to listen instead of trying to figure out what you're going to say next. James 1:19–20 (NASB) says it this way: "But everyone must be quick to hear, slow to speak and slow to anger; for the anger of man does not achieve the righteousness of God."

I've heard stories of some people groups around the world who make use of something called a "talking stick."

When the community leaders assemble to discuss important issues, the head of the council pulls out the talking stick—a short stick ornamented with shells, feathers, or what-have-you. He begins talking. When he finishes, he passes the talking stick to another council member. No one else has permission to talk or interrupt while he holds the stick. This way each council member gets to be heard without someone else interrupting or arguing.

The talking stick may not work for you, but something similar might. The objectives are uninterrupted discussion and careful listening. It is so important for us to be heard.

May I just pause a moment to underline this point? Nothing communicates love and respect in a marriage like a mate who will look you in the eyes, and listen to what you have to say, instead of interrupting or desperately trying to think of a counterargument while you're still talking.

You be that mate.

You be that listening spouse!

It communicates: I want to know and understand your point of view. I may not always agree with it, but I value you and want to hear you. This will go a long way toward resolving the conflict.

> *God realizes it is tremendously important for couples to forgive each other*

5. *Always keep your arguments out of the bedroom.* That's a place for unity and intimacy, not hashing out differences. Don't withhold sex to manipulate your partner. Sex was never designed to be used as a weapon, withheld without mutual consent. "The husband should fulfill his marital duty to his wife, and likewise the wife to her husband . . . Do not deprive each other except by mutual consent and for a time, so that you can devote yourselves to prayer" (1 Corinthians 7:3, 5).

6. *Always stick to the subject.* Most people can deal with only one issue at a time. Unfortunately, some spouses bring two or three issues to an argument, trying to reinforce their point. This confuses the discussion and doesn't aid resolution.

7. *Always deal with disagreements as soon as possible.* The longer a conflict festers, the larger the issue becomes because time tends to magnify a hurt. The Bible says, "Do not let the sun go down while you are still angry, and do not give the devil a foothold" (Ephesians 4:26–27). Anger that has not been dealt with leads to bitterness and even more anger. Never go to bed angry. Why give the devil a foothold in your marriage?

8. *Always decide on a plan.* After the two of you have expressed your points of view and come to an understanding, decide on a plan of where to go from there. That might mean saying some-

thing like, "In the future, we'll discuss how we'll spend our savings before buying—rather than telling each other after the fact."

FORGIVENESS

God realizes it is tremendously important for couples to forgive each other. One of the most impressive characteristics of Jesus Christ was His willingness to forgive. Imagine hanging on a cross and experiencing excruciating agony; yet, praying for those who crucified you, "Father, forgive them for they do not know what they are doing" (Luke 23:34).

When the apostle Peter asked Jesus if he should forgive someone seven times, Christ responded, "not seven times, but seventy-seven times" (Matthew 18:22). He then told a parable about a servant who was forgiven a large debt by his master, but refused to forgive a fellow servant a small debt. Christ describes what happens to the unforgiving servant:

In anger his master turned him over to the jailers to be tortured until he should pay back all he owed. This is how my heavenly Father will treat each of you unless you forgive your brother from the heart. *Matthew 18:34–35*

Genuine forgiveness is a key to healthy conflict and a great marriage. When you have wronged your mate, be quick to sincerely apologize and ask for forgiveness.

MONEY AND MARRIAGE Q&A

Question: My husband and I had been working to pay down debts and trying to save during the past few years, and we actually were doing well and we even built up a nest egg. But then my husband's gambling went out of control, and he not only destroyed our savings, but now we're so behind in our bills that I must go back to work. I was happy and busy being a stay-at-home mom. He's asked for forgiveness. What should I do?

Answer: I know this is difficult, but if your mate asks for forgiveness, be gracious and accept the apology without subjecting him to a series of "I told you so's." This is God's pattern for forgiving and being forgiven. That said, he needs to participate in a gambling recovery program to help him avoid this harmful pattern of behavior in the future.

Answer these questions:

_____ Do you usually ask for forgiveness from your spouse when you are in the wrong?

_____ Are you gracious in accepting your spouse's apology when you have been wronged?

_____ Do you bring up past incidents and use them as a weapon against your mate?

_____ How do you think you and your spouse can improve in forgiving one another?

Remember, maintaining a close relationship with your mate is more important than winning a financial argument. Winning at the expense of damaging your relationship is a defeat. Try to find a solution that benefits you both. And if the two of you can't find a solution to your conflict, seek the help of a counselor.

Our once and for all decision(s) _____

_____

_____

_____

A gentle answer turns away wrath,

but a harsh word stirs up anger.

PROVERBS 15:1

13

CRISIS!

Their friends at church couldn't believe it. Rob and Natalie Fletcher looked like the ideal couple, and seemed to have everything going for them.

But their marriage was unraveling faster than a moth-eaten sweater.

It all started with the housing boom when homes in their area exploded in value. As did so many other couples, the Fletchers sold their modest home and bought a much larger one using a subprime mortgage—requiring no money down and an initial interest-only payment that would adjust in two years. For a while everything ran smoothly.

But after two years, the monthly payment increased by far more than they could afford. Life in their dream house turned into a nightmare. They couldn't sell the home because the real estate boom turned into a bust with house prices dropping.

Bad turned to worse when Rob lost his construction job. They had little savings yet continued their same lifestyle using credit cards. Collection agencies began to harass them and finally they joined the millions of other couples who received notice that the bank was going to foreclose on their home. It was more than Natalie could take. She wanted to end their marriage.

IS YOUR MARRIAGE IN CRISIS?

A marital crisis typically occurs when an unusual amount of stress or unresolved conflict becomes too intense for a couple to manage. A crisis brought on by finances usually involves more than dollars and cents. Anger, resentment, frustration, and hopelessness often control the relationship. Communication becomes increasingly strained—or the two emotionally withdraw from each other. A crisis can be even more challenging when either the husband or the wife contributed to it—rather than its being caused by outside forces—and especially when trust has been broken.

People often react differently to crisis. Our experiences, family backgrounds, values, and personalities influence our response to crisis. Some people react quickly and emotionally, others are more introspective and require time to sort it out. Some retreat and live in denial, while others want to aggressively deal with the circumstances. It is essential to give your spouse the freedom to deal with the crisis in an appropriate way. There is always emotion at this time, and it is crucial for the husband and wife to support each other in every way possible.

Nathan Bridges lost his job and was unemployed for a year. His wife, Laura, recognized the situation was destroying Nathan's self-esteem so she consistently encouraged and affirmed him. On the other hand, Nathan realized Laura's biggest concern was their loss of financial security as their savings vanished. He focused on spending as carefully as possible and working odd jobs to earn money.

Times like this can be defining in a relationship—bringing couples closer together or pushing them further apart. It can become the bridge that moves you from pain to a new level of closeness in your marriage. This may surprise you, but one of the biggest potential benefits is that when people experience a high level of pain, they will change. Impulse spenders often become careful spenders. Credit cards are paid off. Couples begin to communicate at a deeper level. And others become serious about growing in their relationship with Jesus Christ.

WISE COUNSELOR

All couples in crisis will benefit from the counsel of a godly person who can offer objective advice. Some people will panic and make impulsive decisions they regret later. And it is very difficult to make solid decisions by yourself in the midst of a crisis. Proverbs 19:20 says, "Listen to advice and accept instruction, and in the end you will be wise."

I like to think of a counselor as my own personal GPS system. You know—the little device that helps you navigate while you are driving. All you do is enter your current location and the address of your destination, and a color screen guides you there with a moving map and voice directions.

Just like a wise counselor, the GPS system tells you where you are and how to get where you are going. If you take a wrong turn, the little box starts talking to you. "Turn around," it says. "Take the next right and get back on track so you can reach your destination."

The best counselors are concerned people who know Jesus Christ and the Bible well. If you need someone to help you get your finances under control, see the resources on page 167 at the end of this section.

MONEY AND MARRIAGE Q&A

Question: As our debts and arguments exploded, our marriage crumbled. We're headed for divorce unless we can get counsel, but my husband is unwilling to meet with our pastor. Help!

Answer: Some people are embarrassed to seek advice from their pastor. If you know a wise, godly man your husband respects, ask your husband to meet with him. Or I would locate a professional Christian marriage counselor who has a good reputation.

To get your debts under control, log on to MoneyandMarriage.org and connect with a Crown Money Map Coach. If you need debt management, contact FinancialHope.com.

DEALING WITH A CURRENT CRISIS

The severity of the crisis will dictate what is needed to heal the marriage. It is the same concept when you decide what to do when you have been injured. Do you just need a few stitches, is it severe enough to require surgery, or is it a matter of life and death requiring intensive care at the hospital? The extent of the injury determines the treatment.

This chapter will help you evaluate the crisis you may be experiencing. Depending upon the seriousness of your crisis, you have three options to pursue:

1. Moderate crisis—you can solve it with only minor help from others

2. Serious crisis—secure the assistance of a professional counselor

3. Critical crisis—intervention is required

The first step for a couple is to diagnose the severity of their crisis.

You must love and respect each other throughout the diagnostic process. It will require courage and humility, because you need to move toward complete honesty with each other. This can be challenging, because by nature people often don't want to add to an already tough situation, and honesty can be painful. But hard as this life-giving medicine may be to swallow, it leads to healing.

Here are the steps to take:

1. *Pray* together for God's wisdom and direction in your situation.

2. *Agree together on ground rules* for how to deal with the crisis. To help you establish the ground rules review pages 152–156. Include an opportunity for either spouse at any time to call a time-out to pray together, or to suspend a meeting that has

become too intense, when a cooling off period would be of benefit.

3. *Words can help or harm.* Words are easy to cast but difficult to reel in. "A word aptly spoken is like apples of gold in settings of silver" (Proverbs 25:11). Think about how you have been communicating with your spouse lately. Have your words been golden apples or crab apples?

God cautions us against speaking harshly. "A gentle answer turns away wrath, but a harsh word stirs up anger" (Proverbs 15:1). Let gentleness and kindness season your talk. Don't speak when you are in emotional turmoil, because you may say something you later regret. Cool it for a little while; maybe go for a walk instead of talking. But always make sure you come back to the issue, and don't leave it simmering on the back burner. The surest way to de-escalate an argument is to be gentle rather than unkind.

The latest incident may just be a trigger —there may be a deep, long-standing problem that has been buried for months or years

Kindness is like spraying flame-retardant foam on a fire. Take a deep breath, let your face muscles relax, and allow the tension to drain out of your voice. Then, say something that affirms and honors the other person.

4. *Write a letter.* If financial issues have been discussed too often or with too much emotion, it can be enormously helpful to write a letter to each other expressing your feelings and identifying the issues contributing to the crisis. Then meet to pray and discuss the letters.

5. *Identify and confess any sin.* If the crisis has been caused, at least in part, by a spouse, it is healing for the one at fault to confess the sin and ask forgiveness. True repentance—not just sorrow— is what will heal the marriage. The Bible defines repentance as "turning away" from the wrongdoing. For example, if someone is addicted to gambling and is squandering the family income, true

repentance would mean getting the help necessary to break the addiction.

6. *Decide what you will NOT do.* Identify what you won't do to try to cope with the problem. For example, adding more debt to a fragile financial situation often only delays the inevitable, and makes it worse. I have met couples who have taken an expensive vacation to get away from the stress and momentarily substitute pleasure for pain—all funded by credit cards.

7. *Look for the underlying cause.* Be alert for the real source of the hurt between you and your spouse. The latest incident may just be a trigger—there may be a deep, long-standing problem that has been buried for months or years and must be rooted out and dealt with. You may not know where to look for it, but God does. Ask Him to reveal it.

8. *Rebuild the marriage.* In my experience a couple recovering from crisis must be in community with others who can love them and help hold them accountable to make good choices. Many couples on the verge of divorce have enrolled in Crown's financial life group and have had their marriages revived in only ten weeks because a small group of people loved and encouraged them.

We all need others who know Christ and care for us. Over and over again, Bev and I have witnessed the truth of Solomon's words:

> Two are better than one because they have a good return for their work: If one falls down, his friend can help him up. But pity the man who falls and has no one to help him up! . . . Though one may be overpowered, two can defend themselves. A cord of three strands is not quickly broken. *Ecclesiastes 4:9–10, 12*

At any time, if either feels too much frustration or emotional pain or believes they have reached an impasse, he or she should be able to ask to use a professional marriage counselor to facilitate the process. But not just any counselor! Would you pick a brain surgeon by opening the Yellow Pages and stabbing down your finger on the page with your eyes closed? No, I venture to say you would like a few references first. The counselor you choose should be a committed Christian who has a biblical worldview and is experienced in dealing with crisis.

If, however, the marriage is very fragile and there is a high probability it may not survive, then more drastic measures must be taken to preserve and heal the union.

INTERVENTION

Couples experiencing an acute meltdown in their marriage need intervention because they are unable to work out their problems without the assistance of others.

For intervention to be successful, both spouses must commit to be willing to do whatever is necessary to work through the crisis. This could include attending an intensive intervention retreat, marriage counseling, and communication enrichment seminars.

Even though you feel you may not be thinking clearly in such a time of stress, it's vital that you find the *right* person or organization that can provide the most effective help. Select a mature Christian who is a trained professional. To identify prospects, ask for referrals from church leadership and conduct online research to discover what resources are available in your area.

Most severe crises and divorces occur when a couple loses hope that anything can be done to restore their marriage. I realize that there are some circumstances where divorce may occur because of abuse, adultery, or addictions, but most problems can be solved if both partners are committed to resolving them.

SEPARATION AND DIVORCE

A word of caution if you are seriously considering separation or divorce—these steps can be expensive. If finances are tight before a breakup, they can be suffocating afterward, because you are funding two households instead of one.

I simply want you to face financial reality if you are considering separation or divorce. Count the financial cost. Determine how you are going to make ends meet before making a decision that can compound the crisis. As much as possible pursue reconciliation.

Our once and for all decision(s) _____

_____

_____

_____

LOOKING BACK AT PART 4:
SNAGS: COMMON PROBLEMS AND COMPLICATIONS

React: Let's talk about it

1. Describe some of the financial challenges you have faced as a couple. How did you deal with them?
2. Have you and your spouse agreed upon ground rules for handling conflict? What are the most important ground rules you will observe during a conflict with your mate?
3. Is it difficult for you to forgive a wrong done by your spouse? If it is, how will you improve?
4. Review the Bible verses on pages 151–152 that describe the ways we should treat our spouse. If these do not describe the way you are acting, what changes will you make to treat your spouse better?
5. Describe any crisis you have experienced as a couple. What did you learn from it? How can you prepare for one in the future?
6. Share your *once and for all* decisions from the section.

Help!—*Online and other resources*

To help you deal with a crisis

Rosberg Dr. Gary, and Barbara Rosberg. *Healing the Hurt in Your Marriage*. Carol Stream, Ill.: Tyndale House, 2004.

Temple, Mitch. *The Marriage Turnaround: How Thinking Differently About Your Relationship Can Change Everything*. Chicago: Moody, 2009.

Celebrate Recovery is a Christ-based program for anyone who has any kind of hurt, hang-up, or habit. Go to celebraterecovery.com for more information and to find a group near you.

Encouragement from a couple you should know

In the coming years, visual learners around the world will be taught God's way of handling money through a series of short films being produced by Crown Financial Ministries. The first of those films, *Widow and Oil*, was funded by a donation from Bill and Mary DeBardeleben, who are living examples of God's ability to heal marriages.

Before Bill and Mary were married, both had gone through divorces and were now heading toward what they hoped would be a new start in life. But two weeks before the wedding Mary was diagnosed with multiple sclerosis. "For probably the wrong reasons, we decided to get married," Bill says, noting that he hated to abandon Mary. And she wanted to get married because she wanted someone to care for her.

After the wedding, Mary began attending a nearby church. Bill declined to go—until the day that Mary drove into the back of his car. At that point he began driving her to church.

Mary's condition worsened, and her relationship with Bill spiraled downward. She was unhappy in her marriage, but through the influence of a friend at church, she became a Christian. Bill was irritated with her new interest in the Bible, but still, when she asked him to attend a Bible study at the church, he agreed.

Following one of these studies, the pastor invited people to join him for prayer. "I didn't want to go," Bill says. "The next thing I know, I'm kneeling at the altar of this chapel just crying my eyes out. And I remember saying, 'Lord, if You are real, just come in and do whatever You do. Take over, because I can't handle this anymore.' "

After Bill accepted Christ, he and Mary attended a seminar taught by Crown's cofounder Larry Burkett. Larry inspired the couple not only to get their finances under control but to begin resolving their marital challenges. They also established the amazing goal of eventually increasing their giving to 50 percent!

Recently, as the DeBardelebens were considering what to give to a ministry, they each sensed God wanted them to give the largest gift He had ever asked of them. They wanted to be obedient, but to ensure that they were really hearing from God, they decided to write what God was showing them on separate pieces of paper. When they compared the pieces of paper, the numbers were identical. Bill says he and Mary are thankful for a healed marriage and excited to be part of what God is doing around the world.

part five

Times of Your Lives

ENGAGEMENT THROUGH THE EMPTY NEST

Houses and wealth are inherited from parents,
but a prudent wife is from the Lord.

PROVERBS 19:14

14

Before You Say
"I DO"

Karl and Rachael were madly in love with each other. After dating for two years, they became engaged. Rachael thought Karl was the perfect one for her. He was attractive, smart, and fun. She couldn't imagine life without him.

Although they had talked about a lot of different things, finances was not one of them. Rachael had been raised by a single-parent mom, and since money had always been tight, she believed in spending carefully. She just assumed Karl had the same view of money.

During premarital counseling with their pastor, it became apparent to the pastor that Karl might have a financial dark side. He asked them to exchange credit reports with each other and to prepare to discuss their finances at their next counseling appointment.

Rachael was completely taken aback by what she learned. Within the past four years Karl had a car repossessed and declared bankruptcy. Yet again, he was drowning in debt with more than $12,000 in credit card debt, a $15,000 auto loan, $22,000 in student loans—and no money saved. He didn't participate in his company's retirement plan even though his employer offered a generous match of Karl's contribution. He had never used a budget because he felt it cramped his spending . . . and what a spender he was.

As discouraging as his financial situation was to Rachael, what hurt her most was the feeling that she had been betrayed. He had not been honest about his finances.

One of the biggest dangers engaged couples face is becoming so emotionally involved when thinking of marriage that they do not address the issue of money at all. Yet if hidden financial problems surface after the honeymoon, they can destroy the trust relationship of the new husband and wife. I've discovered that men often avoid this honest discussion because their financial problems make them look out of control. On the other hand, a woman may think being in debt makes her appear immature and irresponsible.

> *Be transparent. . . . ignorance about your financial circumstances is definitely not bliss.*

BEFORE YOU TIE THE KNOT

There are four basic things every engaged couple needs to do before their marriage.

1. *Give complete disclosure of your finances*

You should be fully transparent with your financial situation. Make this commitment to each other—no secrets about money! Swap your financial statements that disclose all your assets and debts. Trade credit reports and credit scores and openly talk over any financial stuggles you have experienced. When you are honest—even if there is bad news to deal with—it builds trust with your future spouse. Your fiancé will respect and appreciate your integrity. Remember, ignorance about your financial circumstances is definitely not bliss.

2. *Talk through your financial goals, values, and expectations*

Get to know each other. Learn each other's financial personalities, values, and attitudes. What is it that you want to accomplish in your economic lives as an individual and as a couple? What things are most important to you? The following is a list of questions to help get you started.

- Who is going to be the breadwinner (one or both)?
- If both are breadwinners, what happens when we have children—does the wife stay home to raise the children?
- Are you a hard worker? What career do you want to pursue? What further education will you need?
- What percentage of our income do you want to give? Who do you prefer to give to—church, ministries, the poor and needy, etc.?
- How much of our income do you want to save?
- What is your attitude toward debt? When should we use it? Is paying off debt a very high priority for you?
- Who will handle the bookkeeping and paying the bills?
- How often should we meet to review our finances?
- How do you see us becoming one with our finances? How should we combine our finances? Is there any sense of "my money" and "your money"? If so, how can we overcome this challenge?
- How will we make financial decisions?
- Who will manage the investments, and what is your investment philosophy?
- What are your expectations concerning our lifestyle—what do you want for a home, furniture, cars, clothes, vacations, and gifts?
- What do you think we should spend on our wedding?
- What were your parents' attitudes toward money? How have their attitudes influenced you?
- Do you think my parents or your parents will want to control us by using money? Is there a danger of overdependence on them? If so, how should we deal with this?
- What has your family done for birthdays, Christmas, and gift giving? What should we do?
- To what extent should we help if we have needy family members?
- If we have children, when should they begin to work? What is your philosophy of giving them allowances?

- Do we both know Jesus Christ as our Savior? If not, what should we do?
- Do we both have a solid understanding of what God says about handling money?

Identifying the individual and collective goals is very important for an engaged couple. Review pages 174–177 for the steps on how to do this.

MONEY AND MARRIAGE Q&A

Question: My fiancé has about $20,000 in student loans, and I am completely debt free. After we marry, should I keep my finances separate until he pays off his debt? Or should we combine our finances, which means I would need to continue working to help him?

Answer: When you marry, the Lord wants the two of you to become one in every area including your finances. So, combine your resources and work together to pay off the student loans as quickly as possible.

3. *Develop a spending plan together*

It is a very helpful exercise to develop an estimated spending plan together. Obviously it won't be completely accurate because you will have to make an educated guess at so many items, but you will learn a great deal about each other.

Review chapter 10 for guidance on completing your spending plan.

4. *Learn God's way of handling money*

One of the most important steps an engaged couple can take together is to learn what the Lord says about handling finances. When our children became engaged, the first thing we asked of them was that, together with their future spouses, they enroll in a Crown Life Group; it was a great experience for all of them. Our son Matt said, "In the five years since we married, there have been so many occasions that financial challenges could have led to an argument. But because Michelle and I had learned what God wanted us to do, we were able to simply talk it through."

My suggestion

Now, here's my recommendation: *Don't get married until you do all four of these steps.* I know it will take time and effort to complete them, but you will be glad you did. From experience in working with so many couples, I know you will have a much healthier marriage if you do.

Also, premarital counseling with a qualified pastor or Christian counselor is a must. Proverbs 19:20 says it this way, "Listen to advice and accept instruction, and in the end you will be wise." An experienced counselor knows the land mines newly married couples will face—circumstances you haven't even considered. Securing their advice will be a blessing.

THE WEDDING

The average cost of a wedding in our country is staggering—over $28,000![1] The bride's engagement and wedding rings alone can average two months' worth of the groom's income. Mix today's generation expecting instant gratification, the desire to impress in-laws, and the billion-dollar wedding industry that convinces them to spend endlessly to enjoy one day, and bam!—here's a couple starting their marriage with tons of debt.

I want you to think outside the box and consider another alternative to an expensive wedding.

When our daughter Danielle graduated from high school, Bev and I had the "wedding" talk with her. We told her that someday the Lord might bring the right young man into her life, and they would decide to marry. We wanted her to know what help she could expect from us. We told her we would contribute a certain amount of money for the wedding—not even close to the national average! If they wanted to spend more, they would have to fund it. However, if she and her fiancé spent less than the budgeted amount, we would apply what was left toward the down payment on their first home.

When Danielle and Kyle became engaged, they decided to have a nice wedding, yet do it as inexpensively as possible. They developed a budget and became very creative. A friend from photography class shot the pictures for just the cost of the film. Another friend bought flowers at a discount store and arranged them. A family member sponsored them so they could use a condominium club house for the reception for practically nothing. The food for the reception was catered by a family friend—again, for just the cost of the food. Bottom line, they only spent 35 percent of the amount we promised to contribute—the rest was set aside to add to the down payment on their home.

Surprisingly, the biggest benefit for Danielle and Kyle wasn't the money for the down payment. It was the opportunity to work together on developing a budget and using their creativity to stick to it. It was the beginning of a habit they have continued into married life.

Whatever you do, use a budget to plan for the wedding, decide in advance who will pay for what, and don't use one penny of debt.

THE IN-LAWS

Thomas and Latasha Webb were parents who used money to control their children by attaching plenty of strings to it. Unfortunately, this had not helped their son, Andy, become a mature, independent young adult.

When Andy became engaged to Hannah, the Webbs extended their control to planning the wedding and honeymoon. Hannah was uncomfortable with the way Andy's parents made most of the decisions without consulting her, but was grateful for their generosity.

In the days following the wedding and honeymoon, however,

Thomas and Latasha's domination of Andy and interference in his marriage became unbearable. The choice of the home, furniture, car, and clothes were their decisions, not Andy and Hannah's. Hannah concluded that Andy placed no value on her opinions or feelings because he always followed his parents' wishes. They had violated the *leave and cleave* principle.

In the engagement stage it is important for the couple and parents to discuss this together. As we read in an earlier chapter, God instituted this principle as a basic standard in marriage: "A man shall leave his father and his mother, and shall cleave unto his wife; and they shall become one flesh" (Genesis 2:24 KJV).

During the "leave and cleave" talk, discuss the right way of leaving and how the children can continue to honor their parents in a healthy way. Together, decide how to establish boundaries and how to communicate if the parents step across the line without realizing it.

And lastly, it is an excellent idea for the parents to write a letter to their child and his or her betrothed blessing the new marriage and releasing them. Albert Schweitzer said, "Adults teach children in three important ways. The first is by example, the second is by example, and the third is by example." One of the healthiest ways to be an example of what it means to be godly parents is to let go. Parents can continue to be a terrific source of encouragement and coaching in a young couple's life, but they earn the right to do this by allowing them to leave and cleave.

SELECTING A MATE

There is an issue that can be heartbreakingly difficult to deal with if you have become emotionally involved with a potential mate, and it is this: If you know Jesus Christ as your Savior, God clearly instructs you not to marry someone who does not also have genuine faith in Christ.

The apostle Paul didn't leave much "wiggle room" when he penned this command in 2 Corinthians 6:14, 15, 17:

Do not be yoked together with unbelievers. For what do righteousness and wickedness have in common? What does a believer have in common with an unbeliever? . . . "Therefore come out from them and be separate, says the Lord."

All too often, I have seen the unfortunate consequences of violating this principle. So please take this to heart. The short-term emotional pain of not marrying such a person, pales in comparison to the long-term challenges of not having your faith in common.

Our once and for all decision(s) _____

_____

_____

_____

There is a time for everything,

and a season for every activity under heaven.

ECCLESIASTES 3:1

15

Different
SEASONS

Now that we've been married for more than thirty-five years, Bev and I have experienced the three seasons of marriage: newly hitched, midstream, and empty nesters. Let's examine them all, because each season has its own unique financial challenges.

SEASON ONE . . . NEWLY HITCHED

Mike and Janet Nishimura sat across the table from each other, nervously avoiding eye contact.

"How would you describe your situation?" I asked Janet.

"When we got married three years ago," she said hesitantly, "we were so much in love we didn't think money could be an issue. But it's become our biggest problem."

"Go on," I encouraged her.

"We didn't realize that it would cost so much to live. I guess we didn't have realistic expectations. We never thought we would have so much debt. I thought Mike was my knight in shining armor, and I never thought about having money problems, but . . . we do."

"I understand," I said, nodding. "How about you, Mike? How would you describe the situation?"

He shrugged, speaking in a matter-of-fact tone. "It's really pretty simple. We came from different backgrounds like a lot of couples do, but we never thought we would actually *think* so differently. Janet was used to being able to buy pretty much what she wanted to. I work lots of overtime to make ends meet, but I can't keep up."

The newly hitched season is often the most challenging in a couple's life together. This is why it is crucial to communicate, communicate, *communicate!*

In the Old Testament times, a new husband was to give his undivided attention to his wife as they started their marriage.

> If a man has recently married, he must not be sent to war
> or have any other duty laid on him. For one year he is to
> be free to stay at home and bring happiness to the wife he
> has married. *Deuteronomy 24:5*

In other words, limit distractions early in marriage. I would go so far as to advise not getting a TV or a pet as you begin your marriage! Avoid taking on too many obligations, and definitely avoid spending too much and going into debt. You need to minimize stress, not escalate it. Guard against becoming sidetracked from early marriage's most important priority: getting to know and enjoy each other.

Each season of marriage has three major financial issues. Let's examine the newly hitched.

1. *Lifestyle*

Making the decision to live an affordable lifestyle within your income (living by a spending plan) is part of Destination 1 on the Money Map. Too many young couples make the mistake of financing expensive new cars or furniture. They squander their money on monthly payments that should have been used to begin saving, to get out of debt, or to accumulate a down payment on their first home.

2. *Buy or rent?*

The decision whether to buy or rent a home is major. Typically, you can rent less expensively. If you anticipate staying in your home for at least five years, however, ownership can be a smart choice.

There are two rules of thumb when evaluating what you can pay for an affordable home. First, save enough for a reasonable down payment of at least 20 percent of the purchase price. This eliminates the need to carry expensive private mortgage insurance (PMI). And your smaller payments make it easier to afford larger prepayments, speeding up the day when you can burn your mortgage.

Second, your total housing expenses should not exceed 40 percent of your gross income. This includes *all* housing expenses: mortgage payment, real estate taxes, utilities, insurance, and maintenance. If these expenses exceed 40 percent, you will need to reduce spending in other categories, and that can be more difficult than you think.

Finding an affordable home is challenging in areas where the cost of housing is expensive. If you are in this situation, you can only: save, pray, and wait. Save for the down payment; ask the Lord to provide you with an opportunity to buy an affordable home; and continue to rent until He does.

3. *Wills*

Approximately seven out of ten people die without a will, leaving the state to dictate who receives their assets. Don't let this be you—your heirs will face cumbersome court proceedings and added legal fees, and the estate may be subject to higher taxes. Tragically, under some circumstances, the court can appoint a guardian (who may not be a follower of Christ) to raise your children if you have not named one in your will.

While it's important to have your affairs taken care of, it can be expensive. See if your church can recommend legal counsel to help you with this; sometimes a lawyer will come to a church and provide services for the congregation for a fraction of his or her regular fee.

As Isaiah told Hezekiah, "This is what the Lord says: Put your house in order, because you are going to die" (2 Kings 20:1).

Someday you will die. One of the greatest gifts you can leave your family for that emotional time will be an organized estate. Thirty percent of Americans die before retirement.[1] So don't delay in preparing your will just because you're young.

A popular option to the traditional will is a revocable living trust. Please seek legal counsel before you decide which is more suitable for you.

SEASON TWO: MIDSTREAM

Joshua and Meredith Pierce were trying to do things right. After twelve years of marriage and two children, they were making progress with their finances. They had paid off their credit cards, student loans, and car. The only debt remaining was the home mortgage.

"We're headed in the right direction," said Joshua, "but we don't know what to do now. We want to save for retirement, fund our kids' college, and begin to invest."

"That's right," Meredith interjected. "We're not ungrateful for our progress, but our monthly surplus is only $625. All the things we want to accomplish require a lot more than that. What can we do?"

"I understand your dilemma," I answered. "It's a matter of determining your financial priorities. Let's examine the possibilities."

Saving for retirement

Life expectancy is growing and fewer companies provide pensions. And Social Security? Well, don't bet the farm on it, because the entire system is projected to run out of money. The bottom line: don't rely solely on an employer or the government; *you* need to invest for your retirement.

When investing for retirement, here's a simple rule of thumb: First, take advantage of all employer matches. Second, invest in a Roth IRA.

So, if your employer offers to match your 401k contribution, do it! It's free money. For example, if your employer will match up to 3 percent of your salary in a 401k, put 3 percent in. It's that simple.

If you don't have a 401k match, or once you have contributed the maximum that will be matched, open a Roth IRA at your bank or through a stock brokerage company and fund it. I am a huge fan of the Roth. Although your Roth contributions are not tax deductible, they grow *tax free,* and after age fifty-nine-and-a-half, all withdrawals are *tax free!* The downside of a traditional IRA is that all withdrawals are fully taxable. I believe the government's deficit will lead to much higher income taxes in the future, so using a Roth will be a huge advantage. Log on to MoneyandMarriage.org for more information on the Roth.

You and your spouse can each invest $5,000 to $6,000 every year in a Roth IRA. Since there are limitations based on age and income level, check with your tax preparer to determine what you can contribute.

Saving for college

The average graduating senior has about $20,000[2] in school loans and $3,300 in credit card debt[3] plus what they owe for their wheels. This debt forces some into jobs they would not otherwise choose. They realize too late that "The borrower is servant to the lender" (Proverbs 22:7).

Finding ways to finance a college education is an opportunity for parents and children to grow closer to each other and to the Lord. As soon as children are old enough, pray together each week for God to provide funds for their education. Ask God for solutions that will eliminate or reduce the need to borrow. And then watch! He is eager to reveal Himself to us by answering prayers.

It is a blessing when parents are able to save to help pay for their children's education. There are several educational savings options: state-sponsored 529 Plans and Prepaid Tuition Plans, Coverdell Educational Savings Accounts, and Roth IRAs. Each of these options has pros and cons. Log on to the MoneyandMarriage.org site for an explanation of each along with links to Web sites containing helpful information on student grants and scholarships.

Many parents and grandparents are not in a financial position to fund any of their children's education. If you're one of them—*don't feel guilty!* This may be a blessing in disguise.

When children are old enough, have them work to save for college. When they enter college, encourage them to work part-time, and don't forget summer jobs. When students work to pay for college, they appreciate it more and develop a solid work ethic. Your objective is to have your children graduate with *little* or *no* school debt.

MONEY AND MARRIAGE Q&A

Question: We don't have enough income to save both for retirement and for our kids' college educations. My husband thinks we should put money aside for retirement, but I want to help them through college. What do you recommend?

Answer: Pray together daily for the Lord to confirm His direction to you both. Typically, I suggest saving for retirement as a priority because your children can help pay for their college by working, receiving grants and scholarships, and frugal spending.

Investing

The Bible provides basic guidelines for investing.

The fundamental principle for becoming a successful investor is to spend less than you earn and then regularly invest the surplus. In other words, be a steady plodder. I return to a verse from the Bible that I quoted earlier: "Steady plodding brings prosperity, hasty speculation brings poverty (Proverbs 21:5 TLB).

Nothing replaces consistent, month-after-month investing. Just do it—regardless of the investment climate—because when you do, your investments grow through compounding.

Albert Einstein reportedly said, "Compounding is the greatest mathematical discovery of all time, not E=mc^2." Compounding occurs when the earning your investments produce are added to the principal, then *both* the earning and the principal grow exponentially.

The graph below will help you visualize the benefits of compounding. If a person saves $2.74 a day—$1,000 a year—and earns 10 percent, at the end of forty years the savings will grow to $526,985 and will be earning $4,392 each month. However, if the person waits one year before starting, then saves for thirty-nine years, the result will not be just $1,000 less; it will be $50,899 less! Compounding is your friend, and the earlier you can start it working for you, the better. Start saving today!

Seek advice. If you're not an experienced investor, identify someone who can mentor you—or use a professional investment advi-

$1,000 YEARLY INVESTMENT GROWTH
$1,000 invested each year, earning 10%

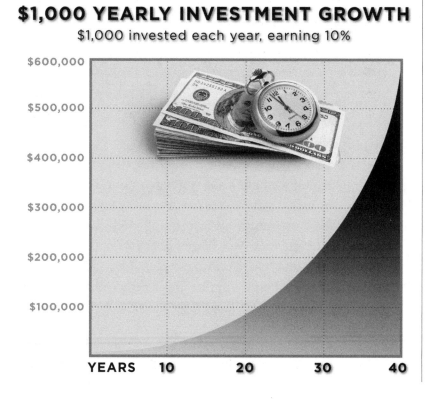

$600,000			
$500,000			
$400,000			
$300,000			
$200,000			
$100,000			

YEARS 10   20   30   40

sor. It is crucial to use an advisor who understands what the Bible says about money, because it will make a difference in the quality of their advice. If you don't know such an advisor, Kingdom Advisors (KingdomAdvisors.org) is an excellent place to search. I suggest interviewing at least three candidates before choosing the one with whom you are most comfortable.

Diversify. No investment is guaranteed; the stock market, bonds, real estate, gold—you name it—can perform well or poorly at any given time. Each investment has its own advantages and disadvantages. Since the perfect investment doesn't exist, we need to diversify and not put all our eggs in one basket. Ecclesiastes 11:2 says, "Divide your portion to seven, or even to eight, for you do not know what misfortune may occur on the earth" (NASB).

> *"Honestly, we never thought we'd get older," Kathy confessed*

SEASON THREE: EMPTY NESTERS

After thirty-plus years of marriage, Sam and Kathy Stephens were empty nesters. Their three children had married and the Stephens were looking forward to becoming grandparents soon.

"Honestly, we never thought we'd get older," Kathy confessed. "Our financial priorities definitely have shifted from raising our kids to preparing for retirement."

"I realize that women usually live longer than men," added Sam. "Kathy is always asking if she will have enough to live on if I die before she does. I want to make sure she's taken care of. We also want to be more generous in funding God's work and volunteering more time to service. We've got pieces of our finances together, but we don't have a real game plan."

"Don't forget that you'll want to spend time with your grandkids once they arrive," I said, laughing. "Let's examine what you'll need going forward."

Preparing for the death of a spouse

I have counseled many widows who understand very little about their finances, and they all have one thing in common. They are frightened. They don't know whom they can trust or what to do with their money.

Both spouses should be prepared for their mate's death. They should have experience paying the bills, adequate life insurance to replace the income of the breadwinner, and full knowledge of their assets and debts. It's also essential that they personally know and trust their financial advisors.

Crown has developed *Set Your House in Order*, an outstanding workbook or CD that enables a couple to have all their financial information in one place.

Investing for retirement

When deciding where to invest, you need to consider your goals, time frame, and risk. The concept of risk is important because investments with the greatest potential for profit also carry the greatest potential for loss—at least in the short run. This means you should invest money differently as you grow older. You should shift some of your money into more conservative investments as you age.

Long-term care

Currently, about nine million Americans age sixty-five and over need long-term care. Most of us think of long-term care as something needed by older people, but an accident or illness can strike at any time. Historically, members of the extended family provided care when needed, but today's families are smaller and often scattered across the country, adding an extra challenge to care for an aging loved one. In addition, people sometimes need care that is beyond the ability of the family to provide. It is wise to talk with an expert on long-term care insurance to determine if this option is right for you.

Remember, in every season of marriage couples should always focus on communicating well with each other and on using Crown's Money Map to work toward true financial freedom. Then, tackle the particular challenges of each season of marriage.

Our once and for all decision(s) _____

_____

_____

_____

LOOKING BACK AT PART 5:
STAGES OF MARRIAGE

React: Let's talk about it

1. If you are engaged, have you completely disclosed your finances to each other? Have you thoroughly discussed your financial goals, values, and expectations? If not, when will you?

2. If you are engaged, do you and your fiancée understand God's way of handling all your money? Have you developed a spending plan for your estimated income and spending once married? If not, when will you?

3. If you're married, in what season of marriage are you? What are the two biggest financial challenges you face? How do you propose to deal with them?

4. Do you have a current will? If so, how did you decide upon how to distribute your assets? If you have children, whom have you appointed as their guardian?

5. What is your game plan to save for the empty nest season of marriage and your retirement?

6. Share your *once and for all* decisions from the section.

Help!—*Online and other resources*

One of the best things you can do as a premarried couple is to learn more about each other's personality and how you will relate to each other. Log on to MoneyandMarriage.org and take the *Couples Personality ID Profile*. It's fun and—we hope!—pain-free!

Crown Financial Ministries has developed *Set Your House in Order,* an outstanding workbook or CD that enables a couple to have all their financial information in one place. Go to MoneyandMarriage.org for more information.

Kingdom Advisors (KingdomAdvisors.org) is an excellent place to search for a financial advisor who will counsel you from a biblical perspective.

Encouragement from a couple you should know

In the early season of their marriage, Don and Liz Meadows were living the American dream—and then some. Their home totaled 7,000 square feet and was designed with an indoor swimming pool.

But in later years, Don and Liz became concerned about the debt they were carrying. In 2004 they sold their home, which they had purchased with a $400,000 mortgage, and bought another. The mortgage on their new home was $170,000.

Later, Liz heard about the Crown Money Map and ordered a copy, and the couple began listening to Crown's radio program. As they put God's financial principles into practice, they increased their ability to survive the unexpected financial storms that families often face.

The Meadows' storm hit when Don's company restructured. He had earned an excellent salary selling custom suits to business executives, but with the restructuring, he stood to lose as much as 40 percent of his income.

However, instead of scrambling to get a handle on their lifestyle, the Meadows were in a much better position to deal with this change. In fact, they are moving toward being completely debt free in several years, even though Don's commission-based income can vary widely from month to month.

Another key decision the Meadows have made in recent years is to begin tithing—giving 10 percent—of their income. As a result, their perspective on money has completely changed.

Don is thirty-eight and Liz is thirty-nine, and they have two children: Allen, eleven; and Amanda, eight. And, as they prepare to move into their forties and another season of life, they are looking at a career change.

Don has been heavily involved in serving in his church, and he is now looking to attend seminary in order to become a full-time pastor. Currently, the couple has no debt other than their mortgage, and Don will be able to work part time while he's in school.

As they near their forties, the Meadows are reaping the benefits of handling money God's way. And though Don's career change may present challenges, he is now positioned to pursue this new direction for the second half of his working years.

Don and Liz say they are no longer impressed with material things and are content with only enough to meet their needs—an amazing change from a couple who once had an indoor swimming pool in their home!

part six

CREATING YOUR OWN

Home Sweet Home

Encourage the young women to love their husbands,

to love their children, to be sensible, pure, workers at home.

TITUS 2:4–5 NASB

16

Stay-at-Home
MOM?

Juan and Jasmine Gonzales met at college.

Do you believe in love at first sight?

They certainly did.

One of the things that had attracted them to each other was their passionate ambitions. Juan was focused on becoming an attorney and Jasmine an accountant. They married just after their senior year, and Juan was accepted to law school.

After Juan's graduation from law school, the couple had $65,500 in student loans, $11,000 in credit card debt, owed $23,000 in car loans . . . and had nothing saved. He landed a job with a law firm, and, as many people did at the time, they purchased a home they really couldn't afford with no money down. For several years, they lived the good life with no thought of paying down their debt. Expensive vacations, a flashy new car, and designer clothes were all part of their lifestyle.

Then something unplanned happened—Jasmine became pregnant. Equally surprising was that Jasmine wanted to become a stay-at-home mom. That is when Bev and I met them.

"I would like to stay home with our child," Jasmine ventured, "but there are several problems. Even with my salary, we're living paycheck to paycheck. How can we make ends meet if I'm not working full time?"

"And I'm the other problem," Juan interrupted. "Frankly, I'm scared. I don't see how we can afford to lose her income. We'd have to change our lifestyle, and that's not something I want to do. Maybe I'm a little selfish."

"Juan, I appreciate your candor. Our children are now grown and married, and here's what Bev and I have discovered. Having all the stuff in the world doesn't compare to the privilege of raising a child. The Bible tells us that children are a gift from the Lord, and we found that they really are."

I continued, "There's nothing better. And if Jasmine wants to stay home with the baby, there is nothing more important that she can—"

"What about you, Bev?" Juan interrupted. "What do you think about Jasmine quitting her job?"

"Well, there are lots of reasons some married women with children choose to work outside the home—extra income or because they just enjoy their jobs. And they shouldn't feel guilty if they do this.

"But in my opinion, unless the family really needs the income, it's wise—especially during the child's early formative years—for the mother to be home while the children are there. As the children get older, a mother can have increased freedom to pursue outside work."

"Well, I haven't even considered the importance of doing a great job raising a child," Juan said thoughtfully. "I've just focused on what I would be giving up. But how can we afford to have Jasmine leave her job and stay home?"

"The first step is to gather the facts and determine how much income Jasmine actually contributes after giving, taxes, and expenses," I explained. "Couples are often surprised to learn that the net income earned by a working wife is not as much as they expected. Let's take a stab at figuring out what Jasmine's will be after you have the baby."

Look at this worksheet.

MONTHLY INCOME AND SPENDING

	Jasmine	Your Situation
2nd wage earner monthly income:	$ 2,700	$ _____
2nd wage earner's expenses:		
Giving	$ 270	$ _____
Federal income tax	$ 675	$ _____
State income tax	$ 135	$ _____
Social security tax	$ 202	$ _____
Transportation to work	$ 21	$ _____
Lunch/snacks/coffee breaks	$ 15	$ _____
Restaurants/convenience food	$ 160	$ _____
Extra clothing/cleaning	$ 25	$ _____
Personal grooming	$ 5	$ _____
Child care	$ 360	$ _____
Total expenses:	$ 1,868	$ _____
Net additional income:	$ 832	$ _____
Net income per hour:	$ 4.84	$ _____

Juan and Jasmine were stunned to learn that although she earned $2,700 a month, her real take-home pay—after they subtracted her current expenses and figured in $360 for child care—was only $832. Based on working an average of 172 hours a month, her net income per hour was $4.84, which was much lower than they expected.

Complete the worksheet to determine your actual income after expenses.

MONEY AND MARRIAGE Q&A

Question: I want to be a stay-at-home mom, but I earn about twice as much as my husband, and we are having trouble making ends meet. What options do we have?

Answer: You will need to cut expenses to the bone and perhaps downsize your home and car. Also, try to find a way you can earn money working from home to help replace your lost income. In the meantime, watch your spending carefully so you can pay down debts and increase savings as much as possible in advance of lowered income.

NOW WHAT?

"You have my attention," Juan admitted. "If it's really important to Jasmine to stay home with our child, how can we make the numbers work? How can we manage?"

"For most people," I answered, "it's a combination of reducing spending, making some significant lifestyle decisions, and figuring out a way for the wife to produce some income working from home."

"Okay, go ahead," Jasmine said.

"Let's take a look at reducing spending. If you're not already using a spending plan—a budget—keep track of everything you spend and ask yourselves these two questions: Do we really need it? Or can we do it less expensively?"

"I can answer those questions right now," Juan said. "We're spending at least $1,000 a month on things that we want but don't need."

"Then here's what's key for you," Bev responded excitedly. "Stop spending on those things and instead use that money to pay off your debts. Follow the Money Map, and pay off as many debts as possible before your baby arrives."

"Bev's right," I affirmed. "Every time you pay off a debt, it means you have to earn less to make it. And Jasmine is closer to being able to stay home."

"What about lifestyle decisions?" Jasmine asked. "What do you mean by that?"

"It means sometimes making tough choices," I answered, smiling. "It could mean downsizing to live in more affordable housing. Maybe selling an expensive car to be able to buy a used one for cash. Looking at your possessions to decide if there is anything that could be sold and used to pay off debt."

"It means selling a bass boat that I don't use more than a couple of times a year. Getting rid of that debt will save us a boatload—no pun intended," Juan said, smirking.

"And I can carve out time to work from home," Jasmine added. "My employer might allow me to work part-time from home. If not, there are some businesspeople from church who have approached me about doing bookkeeping for them. I wouldn't be surprised if I contributed even more to our income than I do now."

Choosing an affordable lifestyle is clearly an important factor.

Jasmine could be right. Some have earned more income after reducing work-related expenses when they decided to work while staying at home. Of course, the financial benefits are not the only factors to take into account. Also consider the physical and emotional demands of working outside the home and how they affect your family.

HERE'S HOW TO PULL IT OFF

Even before David and Sarah Miller got married, they agreed that it was a priority to prepare for Sarah to stay home if they had any children. David was a truck driver and Sarah a high school music teacher. They came to me for premarital counseling.

I explained to them, "Here the key is to financially prepare to have the flexibility of Sarah staying at home when the children arrive. You need to learn to live on David's income alone before you have children. It's that simple. Use Sarah's income for only three purposes: to give, to save, and to pay off debt."

The Millers agreed. They chose an affordable lifestyle that could be supported solely by David's income. They used Sarah's income to give and to get the family in solid financial shape by eliminating as much debt as possible, and by building up as much savings as possible before their first little bundle of joy arrived.

If you follow this plan, at least you have the option of mom staying home. You can prayerfully ask the Lord what He wants you to do, and you have the financial freedom of deciding to stay home with your child or of returning to the work force.

Choosing an affordable lifestyle is clearly an important factor. If housing or the wheels you drive are too expensive, you lose your flexibility of choice.

It is also wise to draft an estimate of your spending plan based on what it will be *after* adding the child. You will have an extra mouth to feed, so ask your friends who have young children for their advice on what additional expenses you can expect.

If you can't stay at home now

There are lots of reasons that it may not be possible at this time to stay at home and raise your children—insufficient income, too much debt, no health insurance coverage if the wife leaves her job, an unemployed husband. If you are in this situation, simply pray, asking for the Lord to make a way. And be faithful to do everything you can to improve your finances by reducing spending so that you can reduce your debt and add to your savings. Consider making significant lifestyle decisions and explore how the wife can produce income working from home.

Our once and for all decision(s) _____

_____

_____

_____

But one thing I do:

Forgetting what is behind and straining toward what is ahead.

PHILIPPIANS 3:13

Do not carry the baggage of hurts and difficult financial experiences with your former spouse and impose them on your new spouse.

LAURA PETHERBRIDGE

17

STEPFAMILIES

Lee and Naomi Schmidt's three years of marriage had been more of a challenge than either had ever imagined. With first marriages ending in divorce, they were in their late thirties and expecting their first child as a couple. Rounding out the family were two children from Naomi's previous marriage and Lee's son, who lived with his mother.

Lee's divorce had been especially bitter. His ex-wife had tried to take everything, and the judge had awarded her a large child support payment. Naomi's ex-husband was far more understanding, but his child support payments had been sporadic.

"*Complex*—that's the word describing our lives," said Naomi. "Just think about it. We're dealing with more children, more grandparents, more in-laws, ex-spouses who can be difficult, financial problems—the list seems to go on and on."

"She's right," Lee agreed. "We also had a lot of emotional baggage we didn't recognize. For example, my ex-wife is addicted to spending, so it's been hard for me to trust Naomi with the checkbook. And I'm probably giving my son too much. I feel guilty for not being his full-time dad. So how do we cut through all this? How do we develop trust in our relationship when we've both been hurt so deeply before?"

I sympathized. "It's complex all right. All of the normal relational challenges and emotionally loaded variables increase exponentially with stepfamilies. But I have very good news. God loves and cares about all families—including yours. He wants your marriage to succeed."

"That's encouraging," Naomi said.

I continued. "And you're right to realize that trust is a vital factor in a healthy stepfamily, especially if you're coming out of a marriage in which there was a lack of it."

Lee and Naomi nodded in agreement.

"I can see that the two of you love each other and want to have a great marriage. So, let's look at some of the most common challenges for stepfamilies and see what we can learn from the Bible to deal with them. Our priorities will be to decrease the level of complexity and increase the level of trust."

Successfully merging a step-family is more like a marathon than a sprint

If the words complex and lack of trust describe the major challenges of stepfamilies, then *patience, communication,* and *honesty* describe how to overcome these problems.

Successfully merging a stepfamily is more like a marathon than a sprint. In his excellent book *The Smart Step-Family,* Ron Deal says it's like cooking with a slow cooker instead of a microwave. In other words, stepfamilies need to employ patience—time and low heat—in allowing each member of the new household to adjust to the changes. This is especially true when working through finances. For example, anyone who has been single for very long will have become accustomed to making financial decisions alone. It takes working together over time to get comfortable with making these decisions as a couple.

COMMUNICATION

After six years of marriage, Melissa ended it. Her trust account had been drained by her husband and his empty promises to quit gambling away their money. The last straw for her was discovering he was having an affair with a woman at work.

Three years later, she met and married Caleb Brown. After only three months of marriage, a collection agency called her at home, demanding payment on a $20,000 credit card debt in Caleb's name.

When Melissa confronted Caleb that night, he said, "Well, I thought that if you knew about it, you wouldn't marry me." He chose concealment instead of transparency, planting seeds of deceit that will, at best, take years from which to recover.

As we've discussed before, it is important for all couples to address their finances before and during marriage. But for stepfamily couples, the need is amplified because spouses often base their money decisions on the experience of their previous marriage. Read this sentence carefully: Do not carry the baggage of hurts and difficult financial experiences with your former spouse into financial discussions with your new spouse. And memorize Philippians 3:13, which says it this way: "But one thing I do: Forgetting what is behind and straining toward what is ahead."

In addition to asking the premarital questions found in chapter 14, ask each other these questions.

1. What are your financial obligations to your ex-spouse (child support, spousal support, other)?
2. How likely are child support payments to increase or decrease in the future? When will they end? Are you responsible for any additional expenses, such as education, for them?
3. When one of us dies, who will receive the assets brought into our marriage? What happens to them when the surviving spouse dies or remarries? What are the financial plans for your children should you die or be unable to work?
4. What expectations do you have for me to support your family?
5. Do you have a retirement plan? If so, how much is in it? Is any part of it obligated to a former spouse?
6. Do you have any financial commitments to your parents, siblings, or other family members?
7. Was your previous spouse a poor money manager? How will we unify our finances?

8. How should we use what we receive in child support? What do we do when we don't receive scheduled child support?

9. Will we both work outside of the home? How will we handle child care?

10. How will we handle the holidays? How do you feel about gift-giving?

MONEY AND MARRIAGE Q&A

Question: According to our divorce decree, my former husband is supposed to pay $1,000 a month in child support. However, he has yet to pay anything. What should I do?

Answer: Contact him to determine if there is a legitimate reason for nonpayment. If there's none, and he simply refuses to pay the required child support, contact your attorney or social services office in your area. Unfortunately, some people will not fulfill their commitments unless they are compelled to.

UNIFYING FINANCES

Although for a host of reasons I normally recommend that couples have just one checking account together, some stepfamilies would be wise to start with "yours," "mine," and "our" accounts.

One reason for this is security, especially for the woman. Many women who have been left destitute after their husband walked out will find it very difficult to give up the security of having something they can call their own. Their trust account needs plenty of deposits. As a new husband proves his faithfulness, her trust will be won and the finances can be completely unified.

CHILDREN

Stepfamilies are created whenever people marry and bring a child or children from a previous relationship. What may feel like an exciting new start for a husband and wife can feel like a loss for children, who enter the stepfamily with their own wounds—and a missing parent.

Think about their challenges. They may have experienced the trauma of their parents' divorce, or the death of one, and the loss of love and stability. Joint custody and a new parent are bound to cause confusion. If they have to move from their home and school, they will also lose friendships. They may even feel the need to compete with the new stepparent for the time and attention they had previously enjoyed from their natural parent.

Children often react to these changes by becoming jealous of the new parent. They may pit one set of parents against the other or develop an unhealthy sense of entitlement.

Juan and Maria Hernandez entered their marriage with two children each. Juan felt guilty about losing primary custody of his children and overcompensated by giving them too much. Maria felt that Juan not only indulged his children but also treated hers too harshly. More importantly, she felt that he put his children ahead of her.

For most couples, two issues never completely disappear in a stepfamily:

1. If I can't make everyone happy, who comes first: my spouse or my children?
2. Do I love my children more than my mate's children?

Share what you've learned about managing money from God's point of view and explain that your family is seeking to live in faithfulness to God's wisdom

These are important keys for developing a healthy stepfamily:

- Your spouse must be your top priority. Divorce recovery expert Laura Petherbridge has discovered that men often put their children ahead of their new wives. This is a tragic error.

- Express love toward your children and your spouse's children equally. You might not have the same feelings of love and bonding for both sets of children, but you can choose to love them equitably. Hold them to the same expectations, discipline each evenhandedly, and distribute financial resources fairly.
- Never poison the children by ever speaking badly of an ex-spouse. Surveys show that this is the number one request of children of divorce.
- Be a student of each of the children, because each is unique and will adapt to the stepfamily differently. Answer this question: What is the best approach to help each one grow into a responsible adult who loves Christ?
- How the "other" parents handle money is an area over which you may have no control. If the ex-spouse indulges the children or uses money to buy affection, it is important to take a unified approach in dealing with the situation.

Teaching children to be money smart

You and your spouse probably have different approaches to teaching children how to handle money. For instance, you may have required your children to earn money by performing chores. Your new spouse may have simply given an allowance.

It is important to agree on an approach to teach children God's way of handling money. Remember the slow cooker—children's habits do not change easily, and you will need to be patient when you teach them money management.

If your children complain about changes in how money is handled, sympathize with their frustration. Explain that you understand why they're upset ("It's another change you didn't ask for, and I'd be upset, too, if I were you."). Then share what you've learned about managing money from God's point of view and explain that your family is seeking to live in faithfulness to God's wisdom. The new system will bring changes to everyone and all family members will need to be patient with one another. Then share your confidence that God's way will work best for your family.

Crown Financial Ministries has developed excellent materials to teach children of all ages. Log on to MoneyandMarriage.org to explore what is available.

FINANCIAL OBLIGATIONS AND THE EX-SPOUSE

Support payments

If you are receiving child support, remember that this money legally is for the benefit of the child and should be used for no other purpose. And when drafting your spending plan, be aware that it is estimated that more than half of custodial mothers with child support agreements do not receive the payments due.

If you pay child support, fulfill your responsibility: "If anyone does not provide for his relatives and especially for his immediate family, he has denied the faith and is worse than an unbeliever" (1 Timothy 5:8). Make every effort to be faithful with your child support payments even if your former spouse does not use them wisely.

Those who pay or receive child support often feel a lack of control over their ex-spouse. You can't force them to pay on time. You can't dictate that they use the money wisely. Learn to choose your ex-spouse conflicts very carefully. Trying to control their spending will likely damage your relationship and isn't worth it. Trust God with what you can't control.

Future demands or requests

It is not uncommon for an ex-spouse to petition the courts for a change in the support agreement. This can be very difficult for a stepfamily. Though it may never happen, it is smart to discuss this possibility and form a plan in case it occurs.

Checklist of things that might need changing

Insurance. You may need to change the beneficiaries of your life insurance policies. It is also wise to review homeowners, auto, and disability coverage to determine if anything needs to be adjusted. Confirm that everyone in the family has adequate health insurance.

Titles. Car titles and deeds to a home and other property may need to be changed.

Wills. Wills should be changed to reflect your current situation. Crown Financial Ministries has a free kit that will help you compile the needed information prior to seeing an attorney.

Debt. A divorce agreement will not eliminate liabilities on debts. If you are liable along with your former spouse for the mortgage or a credit card, you will remain liable as long as the debt exists. Your credit will be damaged by late payments and the lender may hold you responsible if your ex-spouse stops making the payments. It is essential that you try to remove yourself from these joint debts. This may be as simple as closing a credit card account or as complex as refinancing a mortgage.

PRACTICAL FINANCIAL ISSUES
Social Security

If you were married at least ten years and your former spouse has not remarried, he or she may be entitled to a portion of your Social Security benefits. However, when your current spouse becomes eligible, he or she is also entitled to the spousal share. Social Security pays the spousal share to each and does not divide the share between the two.

Pensions

A Qualified Domestic Relations Order (QDRO) may include a court-ordered assignment of benefits to a former spouse of a portion of the benefits scheduled to be received from a pension.

Joint tax returns

Should the IRS audit a past tax return of yours, both you and your former spouse remain equally responsible for any past errors or fraudulent returns.

Refunds

The IRS can withhold a portion of a refund to cover unpaid child support. Standard refund checks are also issued jointly, requiring both signatures.

Tax exemptions

Tax exemptions normally go to the parent with physical custody for the greater part of the year, regardless of financial contribution, unless the custodial parent waives the tax exemptions.

A shared covenant

I don't recommend that couples execute a prenuptial agreement based on the possibility of divorce, because this sows seeds of deep mistrust even before the marriage.

I am in favor, however, of what financial advisor Greg Pettys calls a Shared Covenant for couples whose marriage will form a stepfamily. This is a written agreement designed to clarify emotionally charged issues that may become obstacles to their maintaining a close relationship.

For example, they should agree on how the children will receive an inheritance. If one spouse dies, will the children receive anything? If the survivor then remarries, what impact does it have on what the children will receive from their parent's estate?

A Shared Covenant promotes open communication, clarifies expectations, and can draw a couple closer together. It protects a marriage by agreeing on a plan for future events.

Our once and for all decision(s) _____

_____

_____

_____

LOOKING BACK ON PART 6:
CREATING YOUR OWN HOME SWEET HOME

React: Let's talk about it

1. If you want the freedom of having Mom stay at home, what steps do you need to take as a couple? Describe any changes you need to make in your lifestyle and spending.

2. What options do you have for earning money by working from home? Is there anything you can do to increase what you could earn from home?

3. If you are a stepfamily couple, describe your biggest challenges and how you think they can be dealt with most effectively.

4. What are the most challenging relationships in your stepfamily? What are you doing to improve them?

5. Are you and your spouse unified financially in every area? If not, what needs to be done and how will you do it?

6. Share your *once and for all* decisions from the section.

Help!—Online and other resources

Deal, Ron L., and David H. Olson. *The Remarriage Couple Checkup: Find Your Relationship Strengths.* Nashville: Thomas Nelson, 2008.

Marsolini, Maxine. *Blended Families.* Chicago: Moody, 2000.

Go to MoneyandMarriage.org for effective materials to teach children of all ages to handle money God's way.

Divorce recovery

Petherbridge, Laura. *When "I Do" Becomes "I Don't": Practical Steps for Healing During Separation & Divorce.* Colorado Springs, Col.: David C. Cook, 2008.

LauraPetherbridge.com for outstanding Divorce Recovery seminars

Encouragement from a couple you should know

Accustomed to logging many lonely miles as a truck driver, Mike Marcukaitis had come to rely on his radio as a way to break the monotony of hours behind the wheel. Bound for his next destination, he was tuned in to Crown's radio program when an unexpected voice came across the airwaves. His wife, Sandie, had called  the program and recorded a short testimony thanking God for the many blessings He had showered on her family. Mike was so overcome by her message of thanks that he pulled his truck off the road as his eyes welled with tears.

When Mike and Sandie said their vows in 1999, it was a second marriage for each. The Peotone, Illinois, couple hoped the Lord would bless their union, and He did.

Mike had two boys from a previous marriage, and when the couple later discovered that Sandie could not conceive, they decided to adopt an infant from South Korea. Their new daughter came home to them in November 2003.

In the months leading up to the adoption, Sandie and Mike came to realize that they had entered into the marriage with different expectations. "Mike wanted me to leave my job in sales and become a stay-at-home mom for our daughter," Sandie says. "I wanted this, too, but I handled the finances, and it didn't seem possible to give up my paycheck."

This led to tension in the marriage because Mike wanted the security of knowing their daughter was home with Sandie when he was on the road. Wisely, the couple decided to thank God for

His blessings and to ask Him for wisdom, and He provided. They began tuning in to Crown's radio program and turned to God's Word for wisdom on how to handle money.

They determined that if Sandie left her job to stay home with their daughter, they'd have to completely overhaul their finances and give up many of the things they'd come to enjoy. "We decided to be as frugal as possible and trust God with the rest," Sandie says. "I started buying clothes at yard sales and resale stores and used a lot of coupons."

The couple also began tithing on their reduced income and soon found themselves growing closer together. Clinging to Jesus' promise that He would provide for their needs, they found that each time they were short of money, an unexpected check would arrive, or a needed item would appear seemingly out of nowhere.

When not caring for her children, Sandie has found the time to earn a bachelor's degree and is starting a new job teaching fourth grade at a nearby Christian school, where her daughter will also be able to attend. She has one bit of advice for other moms in her situation: "If you really want to stay home with the kids, you can do it. You'll have to change your lifestyle, but God will provide."

CONCLUSION

Think of all the good Christian books in the world that have been purchased, carried home, put on a shelf, *and never read*. All of that advice, counsel, exhortation, and wisdom . . . locked between two book covers, trapped on a bookshelf, shut away in some obscure corner of your home.

This book could have been one of those.

But it's not sitting unused on a shelf.

It's not, because you—on your own or with your spouse—invested the time in reading these pages, thinking about these concepts, and perhaps even discussing them in your living room, over the kitchen table, or maybe in the car or out on a hiking trail somewhere in God's beautiful creation.

Bravo! Bev and I commend you. By taking that step, you've made the move out of mediocrity and signaled your intention to take strides in your financial standing and in the long-term strength of your marriage.

Just don't stop now! You now know God's way of handling money and enjoying a great marriage . . . but knowing is only half the answer.

You must also do it.

You must put into practice what you have learned.

As I said earlier, here's how Jesus described that dynamic: "Everyone who hears these words of mine and *puts them into practice is like a wise man who built his house on the rock. The rain came* down, the streams rose, and the winds blew and beat against that house; yet it did not fall, because it had its foundation on the rock" (Matthew 7:24–25).

That's a reassuring picture, isn't it? Makes you feel kind of cozy thinking about that well-built house standing strong through all the storms. But in the same parable, Jesus also described a scene that's not cozy at all. He went on to draw a picture of what happens to the one who chooses *not* to apply what he or she has learned.

"But everyone who hears these words of mine and does not put them into practice is like a foolish man who built his house on sand. The rain came down, the streams rose, and the winds blew and beat against that house, and it fell with a great crash" (vv. 26–27).

The Greek term describing the fall of that house is quite emphatic, and could be translated with words like "exceedingly great," high, large, loud, and mighty."[1] It makes me think of a house in the direct path of a killer tornado.

When you think about it, it's not that the second man in the story closed his ears to the Lord's words. He listened. He heard. He may have even taken some good notes! But then he stuffed those notes in the back of his Bible or into a stack of papers on his desk and he never did anything with them.

As it turned out, all of those good, life-giving words did him no good at all. When one of life's storms came roaring across his landscape, his home blew apart like it had been made of papier-mâché.

The fact is, all of us from time to time experience financial and marital storms. But if you have built your house on the rock-solid principles found in the Bible—*and have begun to put those truths to work*—your financial house will not fall, and your marriage will continue to improve and flourish.

So, I plead with you! Make a plan to review these principles, challenges, and discussion questions to keep them current in your marriage. Give generously, save, and get out of debt. Become a faithful steward. Make progress on your journey to true financial freedom. And commit to applying what God says about experiencing a dynamite marriage. Communicate, love, and serve each other, and resolve conflicts quickly. Use your finances to benefit your marriage.

By the way, one of the best ways for you to apply what you've learned is to *teach* others. Bev and I have taught more than fifty Crown small group studies. The people in these groups have made huge progress, but the ones who benefited most were . . . Howard and Bev! The teacher learns more than anyone else.

So take others through this book, or get the *Money and Marriage God's Way* video series and facilitate a small group. One of the best ways to demonstrate your love for your family and friends is to get your finances and marriage in order and encourage them to do the same.

Then, when those inevitable storms come, you *and* your friends and family will enjoy marriages and homes that will stand, lovely, loving, and strong, through all the years God gives us to live.

NOTES

Chapter 2: It's God's Idea

1. Don and Sally Meredith, *2 Becoming One: God Designed Marriage; He Can Make It Work* (Little Rock, Ark.: FamilyLife Publishers, 2003), 63.
2. Dr. Emerson Eggerichs, *Love & Respect* (Nashville: Thomas Nelson, 2004), 16.

Chapter 3: Keeping It Healthy

1. Don and Sally Meredith, *2 Becoming One: God Designed Marriage; He Can Make It Work* (Little Rock, Ark.: FamilyLife Publishers, 2003), 93.

Chapter 4: Viva La Difference!

1. Volume 50 Consumer Interest Annual, 2004. The effect of gender and marital status on financial risk tolerance, Yao and Hanna.
2. Shaunti Feldhahn, *For Women Only* (Sisters, Oreg.: Multnomah, 2004), 79.

Chapter 5: Communication Works

1. Dr. Gary and Barbara Rosberg, *6 Secrets to a Lasting Love* (Carol Stream, Ill.: Tyndale, 2006).
2. USA Today 4/28/06.

Chapter 9: Act Your Own Wage

1. articles.moneycentral.msn.com/CollegeAndFamily/Money InYour20s/

Chapter 12: Conflict Resolution

1. Author Mitch Temple graciously contributed much of this chapter from his outstanding book *The Marriage Turnaround: How Thinking Differently About Your Relationship Can Change Everything* (Chicago: Moody Publishers, 2009). Used with permission.

Chapter 14: Before You Say "I Do"

1. According to costofwedding.com, the average cost of a wedding is $28,732.

Chapter 15: Different Seasons

1. Leonard Hayflick, *How and Why We Age* (New York: Random House/Ballantine Books, 1994), 96.
2. http://articles.moneycentral.msn.com/CollegeAndFamily/MoneyIn-Your20s/HowToBlitzYourCollegeDebts.aspx
3. http://www.nelliemae.com/library/research_13.html

Conclusion

1. Biblesoft's New Exhaustive Strong's Numbers and Concordance with Expanded Greek-Hebrew Dictionary. Copyright © 1994, 2003 Biblesoft, Inc. and International Bible Translators, Inc.

Get Additional Marriage Help and Hope at
MoneyandMarriage.org

To help achieve lasting financial success in your marriage,
MoneyandMarriage.org is available 24/7 to come alongside you as a helpful friend.

MoneyandMarriage.org Features...

- Learn how your personalities can support one another in daily financial decision-making by taking the fun and eye-opening online Couples Personality I.D. profile and Financial Goals Survey.

- Read more Frequently Asked Questions about money and marriage issues.

- Use the convenient Online Links to access all of the resources mentioned in this book.